IMAGINE
& YOU CAN

Davinia Gill

Published by Meades House

Acknowledgments

As I begin to reflect on the writing of this book, there are so many people to whom I want to say "thank you." This book is the result of a team effort, as so many wonderful people have had such a huge role in making this happen.

Thank you Dad for all your love and support over the last 30 years. You have been truly amazing and you are simply the best dad in the world, without a shadow of a doubt. You have always been there for us. I am often filled with awe for you because you are so unselfish and have ALWAYS put us first. I have learnt such a lot about unconditional love from you Dad. Thank you for your love, strength and devotion dad. You are the best dad whom anyone could ever wish for and I love you very much.

A special thank you, to my wonderful step-father, Charles, who has over the last few years been a huge support in my life. Charles introduced me to the power of positive thinking and showed me a new exciting pathway into coaching. If it was not for my step-father, I would not have come across the Coaching Academy and have become a Coach. If it was not for my step-father I would not have written my book. So thank you.

Thank you to my gorgeous fiancé Paul. I am speaking from experience when I say, Imagine & You Can… I imagined the sort of relationship and man whom I wanted and I have now got both. Thank you for all your support and love. I am so grateful to have you by my side. I love you with all my heart and always will.

To my best friend Jen, thank you for being such an amazing friend over the years. I love our friendship, it's so fantastic. And thank you so much for doing such a fabulous job with the design work on my book – you have been sensational.

To all my fabulous friends, especially Gary and Nicola who always seem to be there for me, thank you. And thank you to all my fantastic family who are so loving and caring.

Thank you to my wonderful clients who are like family to me, especially Bev and Chris. You have both been such a superb support, listening to all my ideas over the months. And I am so lucky to have you both in my life. Thank you.

To my fantastic editor, Laura Canning – you have been superb, and done such a tremendous job, thank you.

To Paul McKenna whose fantastic books and inspiring NLP courses transformed my life. Richard Bandler, founder of NLP, without you I would not have mastered my emotions so easily. You are truly an inspiration.

To The Coaching Academy for teaching me to become a wonderful coach, and for letting me use their coaching questions. Thank you for being simply fantastic.

Other inspiring teachers that have truly helped me, with their books and seminars, and I am grateful to; the wonderful Anthony Robbins, Louise Hay, Stephen Covey, Michael Neil, John Gray, Barbara De Angelis, Joe Vitale, John Demartini, Brian Weiss, Depak Chopra, Wayne Dyer and Ed Peppit.

Finally, a big thank you to my readers. I am so grateful that I am able to share with you knowledge and give you tools to help you reclaim your power from within and be in control of your emotions. Enjoy the book and make your life how you want it to be. Imagine & You Can….

Contents

The Proof

Here are what some people are saying after reading the rough early edition of this book.

I have always beaten myself up about the way that I look and I have constantly compared myself to others. But finally, while reading this book, I have had an absolute breakthrough. For the first time in my life I have started to feel good about myself. I am working on my self-talk and feel more positive and happy with who I am.
Katy James

This book makes you think about yourself and your life. I have started setting goals and am far more focused and motivated to get my dream job in TV. Watch this space!
Clare Sampsom.

I used to wake up each morning feeling physically exhausted and emotionally drained. Davinia's formula of self-coaching has really helped me to clear away some of my negative addictions and negative beliefs. Just by reading this book and doing the self coaching, I have been able to get rid of a ton of baggage which was weighing me down.
Janice

Before I read *Imagine & You Can*, my life was out of control. I had had a very turbulent year, and had lost a lot of my self-esteem and confidence due to the effects of an eating disorder. At first, I didn't know if there was anything that could help me return back to being the person that I had been prior to my illness, but luckily, I read Imagine & You Can and it has helped me to regain my confidence and lose my paranoia and worry.

The coaching sessions in the book made me confront a lot of demons, and this really assisted in my progress because I learnt how ridiculous the voices in my head sounded, and was able to confront them.

I no longer worry about things so much and can find ways round the causes of distress and upset. Before I got ill, I had a lot of things that I wanted to achieve, and now I am on the way to achieving them all. I am stronger, more honest about my feelings, am able to feel surrounded by happiness even when I am alone, and my relationships have grown stronger. Davinia does not pollute the mind with commercial theories. Through her book she encourages you to come up with the answers to your problems yourself and carry them through, setting goals and targets that will sustain your confidence and inner strength. What the world believes may not change, but it is who you are deep inside that can change the world!

Jackie

I have finally learnt how to control my emotions and be happy. Imagine & You Can *will make you feel great again about life.*
Sarah Baker

There are so many great things happening in my life since reading Davinia's book. Having written down my wish list of what I wanted to 'Be', 'Do' and 'Have' in life, so many have come true. On my wish list, my 3 top priorities were to fit into a size 10 again, meet the man of my dreams and go travelling - all of which since declaring them have come true. How amazing is that?!

Firstly, my parents gave me some money for my 21st Birthday, so I decided to take a month off my temping job and go travelling. Secondly, whilst travelling,

I not only spookily, started to lose weight but I also, thirdly, met a gorgeous man called Adam. Since returning home, I have moved in with Adam and have finally got down to a size 10! The tips in chapter 9 on eating alkalising foods and how to exercise properly, certainly helped me to lose my excess body fat. It seems like a 'miracle' that this has all happened to me and I know it's because I had clearly determined what I wanted in life. Thank you!

Joanne

My relationship with myself and my boyfriend has improved massively as a result of reading this book. I am learning how to be nicer to both myself and my other half.... Imagine & You Can *is easy to read and easy to use. It will inspire you to be passionate about life again.*

Marianne

I first read Imagine & You Can in a professional capacity, but even before finishing the first chapter I was already applying the advice to my own life. I am now working my way through the book and have already seen an improvement in the way I look at the world.

Davinia's book is clearly written, motivating and very effective at breaking down all those negative and damaging thoughts to which we are all susceptible. It's a book I will keep handy and always dip into every so often, to remind myself that I can be the person I want to be. Recommended for anyone who wants to live their life to the full.

Laura Canning (My Editor of Imagine & You Can)

Imagine & You Can will ensure you feel fabulous every day!

Enjoy Reading!

Introduction

In this Chapter you will:

- Learn how to use this book
- Understand how the self-coaching and exercises will transform your life
- Appreciate the idea behind this book
- Imagine and you can

THIS BOOK WILL make a huge impact on your life – guaranteed! As soon as you start this easy step-by-step guide to changing your life, you will be inspired to start making positive changes, today. You will feel better and better about yourself and become happier and more fulfilled, as you learn different strategies and techniques to help you have more positive feelings. This book will help you to be the master of your emotions.

Everything you do in life relates back to your feelings

💜 You have relationships because they give you pleasurable feelings.

💜 You have hobbies because they give you feelings of joy, passion and fun.

💜 You want material things not only because they are useful to you, but also because of the feelings they give you, of pride, excitement or joy. Ok, so you might *need* a new handbag or pair of jeans, but do you really *need* to spend a small fortune on expensive designer ones? No of course not! But you do this because you want them and also you associate them with pleasurable feelings.

💜 Wanting to look fantastic and slim is about wanting to have pleasurable feelings. When you look good you feel more confident and so you have high self-esteem and feel great. Looking good is important. (Although I do think the media focuses on this too much which contributes to many girls' insecurities. Stop thinking 'waif-like' figures and 'flawless airbrushed faces' are a 'must'. They are not.)

💜 Wanting more money to do what you want, such as holidays, going out with your friends, or buying something you want, is about wanting to feel good and have enjoyable experiences.

Everything we do in life is to get more of the good feelings that we want

We buy nice things, or we diet to be slimmer, so that we feel good about ourselves. However, the best feelings will always come from within ourselves. Just think how great it feels when you are kind to a complete stranger or when you help someone in need. Remember how wonderful it feels when you listen to your friend and are there for her completely. The best feelings come from knowing that you are a good honest person who has a high priority for love. When you love yourself and others, unconditionally, then you have truly mastered your emotions.

Unfortunately, many of us can't manage our emotions or create positive feelings from within, in this way. This usually leads to destructive behaviours, as we turn to outside sources to make ourselves feel better, such as over-indulging in or abusing alcohol, drugs or food, or shopping compulsively or gambling.

Is this you? And if so, are you starting to find that these vices are making you unhappy and unhealthy? Do you want to get rid of these emotional crutches and bad habits? Do you want to learn how to feel fabulous at the click of a finger?

By using this book you will learn successful and positive strategies to help you to create more of the good feelings in life. You will increase your levels of confidence, happiness and self-esteem. You will be able to create more of the good feelings you want from within. *You will be able to do this and to change your life.*

How to use this Book

Imagine & You Can is divided into ten chapters. Each chapter has been carefully designed to help you to master an important feeling that will positively make a difference to your life, such as love, gratitude, motivation, happiness, confidence, compassion and wellbeing. You will probably realise that these are all very positive feelings. And just think how amazing it will be to experience them every day of your life. Wouldn't it be fantastic to have control over your mind so you can feel incredible every day? *Well you can.* Let's start now.

The first chapter will help you to understand the power of your thoughts, and help you realise how much your negative beliefs and thoughts are holding you back. But more importantly, you will then learn a fantastic strategy to transform these negative feelings to ones that make you feel wonderful. Sounds simple? It is!

The following chapters will reveal to you how to master all the emotions detailed above. You will learn to love yourself and feel incredible. By using the self-coaching and exercise sessions you will overcome any low self-esteem and unnecessary addictions. By working on yourself, you will make a positive difference to your life.

How the Self-Coaching & Exercises will work

Each self-coaching and exercise section will enable you to master the positive feeling that you have just learnt in that chapter. These sections will help you to get where you want to be, by focusing on your goals and coming up with an action plan. The exercise sections will enable you to use the knowledge from this book and your own inner wisdom to transform your life. They will help you to uncover your own ideas, perceptions and values. This will stop you accepting my opinions and ideas without putting them to the test for yourself first. It is all too easy for us to take others' ideas, perceptions and values without really checking they are right for us. The self-coaching sessions should take around 30-45 minutes each, to ensure you have enough time to find ways of getting more of the amazing feelings you want.

I would suggest that you limit yourself to one chapter a week. What is repeated one day at a time, over many days, becomes a habit. Good habits can be created one day at a time. Once you have re-focused your mind to allow it to get more of the feelings that you want, then go on to the next chapter. Throughout *Imagine & You Can,* use the exercises to re-focus your subconscious mind and positively alter your feelings, so that you will feel good, on a day-to-day basis.

We make sense of the world through both our conscious and our subconscious minds. Your conscious mind is what you actively think with, all day long. It can only hold a handful of ideas and bits of information at any time. Therefore, most of your life is run by your subconscious mind. This stores all your memories and is the source of your creativity. It also runs programmes of automatic behaviour that you use to live your life. These programmes (habits) are incredibly useful. You do not have to consciously think about how to do things, once your subconscious mind has learnt it. For instance, once you have learnt how to tie shoelaces, your subconscious mind remembers how to do it. This is the same with brushing your teeth, putting your clothes on, swimming, driving and many more tasks.

Once you have learnt how to do something and have practised it consciously several times, it becomes a habit and your subconscious mind will then remember how to do it, without your having to think about it. This is great, as it frees our conscious mind to learn new skills and absorb information. Unfortunately, the subconscious mind also remembers your bad habits, such as eating excessively or smoking. This is because you have practised them too many times and they have become subconscious memories. This is the same with negative feelings. If you habitually think bad things about yourself, or are unhappy, this is because your brain is wired in an inappropriate format. Using the exercises in this book will allow you to change your current unhelpful habits and feelings, to ones that will help you feel great. By knowing what you want to feel like, you can do this. It's as simple as that!

The Idea Behind this Book

Do you remember when you used to daydream and go into your own little fantasy world? Think back to those times when you would allow your mind to wander and you would create all sorts of exhilarating stories and scenarios in your head. Do you still do that? You probably know that most of your best ideas come to you when you are in this "daydream" state. If you really start to use your imagination and think about what you want, then you will find a way of making this happen. When you want something enough, you will find a way of turning your dream into reality. The magical part about being a human being is that we have fantastic imaginations. If we can create something in our minds, then we can make it happen in our lives.

Everything in this world, from furniture to cars and houses, has come from people's imaginations and daydreams. By using your imagination, you can create all sorts of ideas and wonderful dreams that you can make reality.

One day, while I was daydreaming and in my most creative state, I started to think about what I and so many other girls and women would like to have more of in life. It's more joy, and more control over our emotions. There are eight feelings that I consistently cover with my clients that I am sharing with you in this book. If you had less stress, doubt, anger, fear, loneliness and worry and more happiness, love, confidence, motivation, excitement and good health, you would be far more fulfilled. This then sparked the idea for this book.

Over the last few years, I have researched fully into each emotion and how to get more of it. I have spent numerous hours on coaching courses, NLP courses, reading books on how to be more confident, how to have better relationships, how to be more motivated, happy and so on. I have spoken to countless people, who are the very best in each area, to give me more understanding and knowledge on how to experience more of each feeling. The key is to focus on what you want to experience and come up with ways on how to do this, by copying other people who are successful in these areas. This is what I have done to create more of the wonderful and positive feelings in life. By being curious and hungry for knowledge on how to feel great, I have come up with numerous ways for you to experience more joy in your life. *Imagine & You Can* will give you the answers and impetus to get more of the good feelings in life.

Thoughts and ideas with the necessary actions can turn our dreams into reality

This book is exactly what it is called: *Imagine & You Can*. Imagine that you can do something and you can. We are all too caught up with why we can't do something, so that we don't disappoint ourselves if we fail. But surely, it would be far better to imagine something fantastic for your life and then to make it happen? Imagine – and you can!

One of the favourite questions in the "self improvement" industry is "What would you do if you could imagine that you cannot fail?" This question doesn't inspire me at all, as it has the dreaded "fail" word. It automatically sets you up for failure. Don't think about failing. There is no such thing as failure, only feedback. If you don't get it right the first time, then at least you will have obtained some valuable knowledge on how to do it better. Imagine that you can do something… what doors does that open?

Imagine yourself being happy and you will. Imagine that you have that perfect relationship and you will. Whatever you want you can have. I know this to be true just from writing this book. When I first set out to do it and told my friends, one of them asked how I could write a book without having any experience. I am a personal trainer and coach, not a writer, so at first I found this feedback disheartening. Was my friend right? Why would people want to read my book when there are so many other books out there with similar messages?

But then I found myself turning this negative attitude around to something far more positive and empowering. I said to myself, "Yes, but imagine if I can do it! Imagine if I can help others to get the life that they want. Imagine if the book became a bestseller." Once I imagined it, there was absolutely no stopping me! And now you are holding the book in your hands. I imagined I could – and I did.

But, if I'd listened to my friend I would have given up before even writing one chapter.

Yes, there were a lot of hurdles for me to overcome, and I had to work hard to get down on paper what I wanted to say. But all writers have to start somewhere, and that is exactly what I kept telling myself. This then gave me the inspiration and impetus to leap over the first hurdle and start writing my book. So my very important message to you is that if you want something enough, you can have it. Imagine yourself doing it, achieving it and you will get what you want. Imagine & You Can!

P.S. Please note for obvious reasons, throughout the book, when I refer to how my friends and clients have changed, I have not used their real names.

P.P.S. Wouldn't it be amazing if after you have read this book you are in control of your feelings and start living the life you want? You will…

Chapter One

Understanding the
Power of Your Thoughts

*To believe you can do something or not believe
you can do something, that is the question.*

*A belief is: an acceptance that something exists
or is true, especially one without proof.*

In this Chapter you will:

- Understand the power of your thoughts and beliefs

- Banish any bad beliefs about yourself

- Reshape and change negative beliefs to ones that
  support you

- Direct your mind and thoughts to create the life
  that you want

The Power of Your Thoughts

Understanding your own thoughts, and learning to consciously control them, is essential to achieving your dreams. The power of your thoughts is immense and can affect not only you but all those around you too.

Imagine if Alexander Graham Bell hadn't believed he could make a device that would enable someone to listen to others and to talk into it? You wouldn't be able to telephone somebody on the other side of the world. If Alexander Fleming hadn't thought that there was a cure to kill bacteria in our bodies, then we would not have penicillin. If Walt Disney hadn't thought about creating cartoon characters, we would not have the wonderful Disney films and theme parks. These are just a few of the many examples of how the power of our thoughts can affect the world.

Every thought we have, and every dream we imagine, can be turned into reality with the necessary action. And this is true for both positive and negative thoughts and dreams.

Think about people you know. What do they consistently think about and how do these thoughts then show up in their lives? Do any of them constantly talk about not having enough money? If they do, this will no doubt be because they don't have enough. And this thought will manifest in their lives.

You can see this in anyone's thoughts. Whatever people feel they have or haven't got in life, they will experience. Do you know anyone who continually worries about being ill? I bet they are probably ill a great deal of the time. That is the power of their thoughts. Do you know somebody that is positive and upbeat? Does this person seem to be happy most of the time? Does this person have fantastic results in most of what they do? What this person is feeling they will experience in life. These are all examples of the power of thought in action. The idea of 'positive thinking' isn't just a phrase – it can affect how you see things and how you live your life.

Understanding and learning to consciously control your thoughts is vital and necessary to achieve your dreams

The reason why most of these people are in the situations they are in, is because their thoughts and beliefs have attracted and created these situations. Everyone with the ability to think is literally creating something every minute of every day. Whatever you focus your thoughts on will become reality in your world. If you are constantly having negative thoughts, they will not help you to achieve the life you want. An uncontrolled mind can turn a neutral moment into a painful moment. It can turn nothing into something. It can create misery where there wasn't any before. But, by simply changing these negative thoughts to positive ones, *you will change your world*. Have positive thoughts and you will be able to create the life that you want.

The Power of Your Beliefs

Our beliefs affect how we feel and who we become. Beliefs are the thoughts and ideas that are no longer questioned by us. If you continually tell yourself such as "I am ugly, I am fat, I am lazy, I am not a morning person" and so on; you will start to believe it. Unfortunately, too many of us are saying things like this to ourselves, too often. And so, we are giving ourselves ongoing bad feelings.

Maybe you have also heard others say similar things to themselves, or to you, so that you believe them. These limiting beliefs will hold you back and affect who you are and who you will be in the future. And once you get into the habit of thinking about yourself in a negative way, you will do it automatically unless you recognise it and learn to stop.

Why is it that two people living in the same world, with the same set of circumstances, the same background, can experience life so differently? This is simply because of their beliefs. When we are willing to change our primary belief structures, then we may experience a true change in our lives. Beliefs have the power to create or destroy your life. Every thought, idea, expectation and action is the direct result of your beliefs.

If you believe that you are a happy person, then you will be happy

As a child, I always wanted to be an actress. I loved acting and putting on a show for people. I was outgoing, creative, flamboyant and I loved to entertain people. Every Sunday afternoon, a friend would come over to play, and without fail we would create a play to act out for my family. Nothing gave me greater pleasure. I had always believed that I would be an actress. I was convinced that I would live out my dream, until one day I allowed my belief to be totally shattered by another person.

At the age of ten, I vividly remember sitting in class, daydreaming about becoming an actress. My teacher noticed that I was not working and came over. I stupidly told her that I was daydreaming and then told her what I was thinking about. Naturally, she was stern and told me in a patronising tone that I would be far better off concentrating on my maths and forgetting about my little fantasy. I distinctly remember her repeatedly saying it was impossible for me to become an actress unless I came from a very rich family or had connections in the industry. Neither of these comments were true, yet I naively believed what she said. The seed had been sown; I thought I would never be an actress.

A few years later in an English class, we were told that we had to give a talk the following week about a hobby. I remember feeling incredibly nervous and having butterflies in my stomach before the speech, which was strange, as I had never had an issue with talking to groups of people. But because a lot of my friends were scared about public speaking, I started to take on some of their fears. By the time I actually did my talk, I was a nervous wreck. When I started to speak, I began stuttering. Some of my class mates then laughed at me, which caused me to not only feel very uncomfortable but to stutter even more. The experience was horrible and I decided from then on that I would never be able to stand up in front of lots of people and speak and so, I couldn't be an actress. My passion for acting had been squashed. I had given up on my dream.

Looking back on it now, I know I shouldn't have given up so easily and I shouldn't have listened to others. I should have believed in myself, but I was young and I thought that my teachers knew best. So of course, I took what they said on board, and I believed them. I listened to what others said, but actually what the truth was, and what I should have said to myself, was "What do they know?"

What I know now is that all actresses have to start from somewhere. How do the Angelina Jolies, Gwyneth Paltrows and Jennifer Anistons of this world get to where they are? By simply *imagining what they want and taking massive action to get there*. Remember, people often advise us and foist their opinions on us, thinking they know what's best for us. These comments can often conflict with your dreams. So, dismiss them. Don't believe them because you will then take their belief system into your own. Don't ever give up on your dreams.

Direct your mind and thoughts to create a life that you want

If you have the wrong beliefs, these will stop you getting what you want. Your beliefs often come from other people, parents, teachers, friends, family and the media. You come to accept these beliefs as absolute truths.

Think back to your childhood. How were you affected by what someone else said? Did you have a harsh comment from a teacher or friend such as, "You are so clumsy!" or "That was a stupid thing to say!" How did that make you feel? Did you then form strong beliefs about yourself?

It is very likely that those beliefs will still affect your behaviour today. If a teacher told you that you were clumsy, every time you drop something now, you probably still hear that teacher's voice. That is a belief, and sometimes beliefs can be incredibly disempowering. What negative beliefs do you have about yourself? What beliefs have stopped you striving for what you really want?

If you have beliefs that are holding you back, you need to change these straight away.

I know over the years you have probably told yourself time and again that you can't do something. In fact, you have actually programmed yourself to believe that you can't do something. But the good news is that you can! If you think you can do something you will be able to do it, but if you think you can't do something then you won't.

Neuro-Linguistic-Programming

What you imagine in your mind and the things that you say to yourself affect how you feel. When you imagine terrible scenarios in your head and talk to yourself in a negative way, then there is no doubt you will feel bad. If you imagine nice things happening and talk kindly to yourself, then you will feel good. Be your own best friend.

In the mid 1970s, Dr Richard Bandler and John Grinder started to explore this relationship between how we think, how we communicate both verbally and non-verbally and our patterns of behaviour and emotions. This study led them to come up with the revolutionary idea of Neuro-Linguistic-Programming (NLP). NLP uses positive ways of influencing people and helps them change negative thoughts about themselves, in an instant. NLP helps you to understand how your brain is wired and, more importantly, how to reprogramme it and change any unwanted behaviours and beliefs.

I heard about NLP on self-development courses, and knew immediately that this was something I had to learn about. So I attended one of Paul McKenna's NLP courses, and, literally within one week, I learnt how to take complete control of my mind and achieve positive feelings. By the end of the course, I understood the power of my thoughts and beliefs and re-focused my mind. And even more importantly, by the last day of the course, I had amazingly eliminated all my negative beliefs on public speaking and stood up on the stage in front of 500 people and spoke. It was exhilarating.

It was from then that I realised by changing my limiting beliefs and thoughts I could do anything I wanted. You must not underestimate the power of the mind. By thinking about what you want to feel like, look like and do in life, you can achieve it.

Impact of your Belief on Others

Have you ever experienced a time when you thought you couldn't do something but your friends and family believed that you could, and that made you feel more confident? At school were you convinced that you wouldn't pass your exams but because your parents consistently encouraged you and believed that you could, you too started to believe in yourself, and then you did well? Have you ever believed in a friend when she doubted herself, but by you giving her support she was able to overcome her insecurity? The power of positive beliefs can do wonders, so remember to encourage others, as well as yourself.

Think about the story of the first four-minute mile. For years, people believed that it was impossible for a human being to run a mile in less than four minutes, until Roger Bannister proved them wrong in 1954. Within one year, 37 runners also beat the four minute mile belief; the next year, over 300. That is the power of positive beliefs.

This also works with the placebo effect. When people are told a drug will have a huge benefit, they will mostly experience that benefit, even if they are given a sugar pill instead of an actual tablet. These people believe the 'drug' will work, and so it does. That is the power of belief.

I saw this recently when I was working on a confidence-building session with a group of sixth formers. During the session, I asked one of the students to read a passage from a book on confidence to the rest of the class. He hesitated for a few moments, then took the book and started to read. After he had finished, a couple of the students clapped and smiled at him. I'd never seen other students applaud someone just for reading aloud but thought it was probably just camaraderie and I carried on with the session. But after the class, the teacher came over to me with a beaming smile and explained that the particular young man never read aloud in class because he had a bad stutter. In fact, his mother, who was a dinner lady at the school, has always asked the teachers not to make him read aloud so he wouldn't be embarrassed.

But I hadn't known this and so I'd asked him to read and had no idea that he couldn't. Because I believed he could, he believed he could. And he did!

Although his mother was trying to protect her son in asking teachers not to ask him to read aloud in class, this was indirectly having a negative affect on him and reinforcing his own belief that he couldn't do it. The teachers never asking him to read aloud either also reinforced this belief. But he could and did, do it.

This is an important point to remember - the impact of *your* belief on *someone else's* abilities will affect the beliefs they have about themselves, and so affect their performance. Always believe in others and support them to help them along in life too.

Banish Bad Beliefs

Eliminate all your negative beliefs now and you will get the life that you deserve and want. It really is that simple. Negative feelings are reinforced by repetition of the thoughts that trigger unhappy feelings. If we stop repeating them, the feelings die. That really is it.

Our brain is a mass of millions of neural pathways. Every thought, belief, feeling and action that we take creates new connections. Each time we repeat one of these thoughts or actions, that specific neural pathway is reinforced. Each neural pathway gets physically bigger through repetition and this is how a habit is formed. Every time we repeat that behaviour, we strengthen that neural pathway. As you practise positive thoughts and beliefs, your neural pathways will grow and being positive and happy will become second nature to you.

All successful and entrepreneurial people, such as Bill Gates, Sir Richard Branson, Sir Alan Sugar, JK Rowling and Paul McKenna have a solid belief not only in themselves but in what they do. By having a strong belief in yourself, you can overcome any hurdle in life and also shape your own destiny.

Some Important Beliefs:

- Believe in yourself
- Believe in the power of beliefs
- Believe in your imagination and the power of creativity
- Believe in making a difference
- Believe in being happy and having fun
- Believe in being grateful and helping others
- Believe there is no such thing as failure, only feedback and outcomes
- Believe you can do it
- Believe in living life to the full

These are, of course, positive beliefs. But, now that you know how beliefs and thoughts can affect your life, you can get rid of, or reshape any negative ones that are holding you back. Try the exercises on the next few pages to get started.

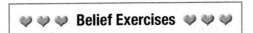

EXERCISE ONE

What beliefs guide you?

Example: "I must always be on a diet to be thin" or "it is impossible to become an actress as there is too much competition."

My fault that Eve does not have a good dad due to picking a man who is not a good father.

Which beliefs hold you back?

Example: "I can't become thin because I don't have the discipline"

I cant progress caree wise as I am not smart enough & will always need to be under someones guredence.

What do you need to believe about yourself, to get the life that you deserve?

*That I am very capable & have many
skills. That I deserve to take part in
things & make an effort with myself just as
much as anyone else.*

EXERCISE TWO

Make two lists for your beliefs:

Beneath are two lists for your beliefs. One list is for your empowering beliefs such as
"I am fun to be with", "I am sporty," "I am lucky," and one is for your disempowering
beliefs such as "I am stupid," "I am fat", "I have horrible arms". Write in the appropriate
columns your beliefs about yourself.

EMPOWERING BELIEFS	DISEMPOWERING BELIEFS
(the ones that push you in life and make things possible for you)	(the ones that hold you back in life and limit your options)
I am a good mum	' I am not that bright.
I am a lucky mum	' I am not pretty.
I am liked/loved by f&f.	ˉ no one ever fancies me.
I am a good friend.	' I have horrible boobs.
I give a lot to people.	- I cant do things - I
I am a good listener.	dismiss them for no reason.
I can be fun.	' I make no effect
I	as feel its pointless (Makeup ed)

EXERCISE THREE

Reshaping & Changing Negative Beliefs

Identify the belief that you want to change. Think about and feel the negative consequences that you have experienced because of this belief. Ask yourself, and write down, what the belief has cost you in your relationships, your physical body, your health, your finances and your level of happiness?

It stops me in all areas. stops me leading a full life sometime - new hobbies - meeting people. Which in turn makes me feel low / isolated /over eat / moody. Not consistant in what I want to do / achieve - Job - feel I am a het down as dont push myself.

💙 How much does this belief cost me every day?

Varies but is always there.

💙 Look ahead 5 years. How much does this belief cost me now?

Still in same position - same job - same non relationship - still very little hobbies / intrests / social life. limits my world - impact on E too.

💙 Look ahead 10 years. How much has this belief cost me now?

As above - Wasted years - could be expnence new enjoyable things & meeting new friends / living / - life just past me by!.

Realize that if you don't change your beliefs now, then this could happen to you. You have a chance to change it now.

Ask yourself, what am I going to believe about myself *now* that will be empowering? Write them down stated in the positive.

*Ask myself what do I enjoy? What I want to experience
& go do it - Do not make any excuse -*

Close your eyes and think, how will these beliefs transform the quality of your life, by answering the following questions:

❤ What will I gain by having these new beliefs?

*new friends / new experiences / feel
happier / feel more forefilled / more in Control
less angry - frustrated - upset - depressed.*

❤ Why will I be happier?

*Not plodding along Doing what I want
to deep down & going for it. Not
being put off by failing / Anxity, Having a
life - better & more forefilling*

❤ How will my relationships be better with this belief?

*Happier me = better mum
attract positive people.
be a better friend / fam member.*

❤ How will I be more financially successful with this belief?

*May lead to ↑conf = me more
likely to push myself more Caree
wise & go for it .*

💜 How will my body be transformed with this belief?

look after me as happy - settled.
no emotional eating. No abusing body
with crap food.

💜 Look ahead five years with your new beliefs and ask yourself, how has my life improved? What have I done because of my beliefs?

Lived - became more content / happy / confident.
Expirenced loads instead of missing out.

💜 Look ahead ten years and ask yourself again, how has my life improved? What have I done because of my beliefs?

As above. Hopefully taken control of my
life.

💜 Look at both futures and decide which future you want.

_:)_

💜 Write down your new beliefs. Repeat them ten times a day - minimum. Read them out morning and night.

I can do anything - I am just as
important as anyone else & intitled
to do things. I deseve a life.
There is No reason why I can not do
things that make me happy.

Remember - by changing your beliefs and having more empowering ones that support you, you will be able to achieve what you want in life.

Chapter Two

Love Yourself & Increase Your Self-Esteem

To love or not to love myself, that is the question.

Love: an intense and deep affection, fondness, tenderness, warmth, intimacy and attachment.

In this Chapter you will:

- Eliminate any negative behaviours and bad habits
- Think positively about yourself
- Treat yourself with love and respect
- Feel great about yourself

One of the biggest truths you need to realise is this:

You must love yourself to live a happy and fulfilling life, because if not, you'll feel miserable and alone.

But the real truth is that most of us don't love ourselves. Like most people, you probably spend your days rushing around trying to please others, trying to fit your daily chores around this and never making enough time for yourself. Maybe you try to "be there" for other people and aim to have fantastic relationships with your partners, family and friends - but probably not yourself.

Like so many of us, when the going gets tough or you get bored, you probably rely on outside distractions like food, alcohol, cigarettes, shopping, watching TV… anything to make you feel good. So many of us are finding our addictions and negative behaviours, from eating disorders to shopping addictions, are repeatedly cropping up to give ourselves some instant pleasure – as we don't know how to create it from within.

Is this something that you can relate to? Do you take good care of yourself or do you, like most other girls, harm yourself with damaging comments and negative behaviours? When you look in the mirror are you happy with what you see – or do you instantly put yourself down? Do you know how to create inner joy – or do you need the outside world to make you feel good?

What would it feel like to wake up every morning and be happy with who you are? Imagine every day looking in the mirror and smiling at your reflection because you are secure in who you are. How good would that feel?

After this chapter you will love yourself more and you will feel so much better about yourself – just read on…

What is loving yourself?

When you love yourself you cherish yourself. You respect yourself and set yourself high standards. You do not abuse your body with too much food, excessive alcohol, cigarettes or drugs. You take care of your body. You exercise to remain healthy and strong. You say good things about yourself and others. When you love yourself you don't need to compare yourself to others. You are happy in your own skin. When you love yourself you do everything possible to look after yourself and others.

With this description in mind, decide if you really love yourself enough:

💜 Do you like yourself?

💜 Do you feel, both in your mind and deep down inside, that you are a good person?

💜 Do you look after yourself properly?

♥ Do you always say good things to yourself?

♥ Do you look in the mirror and only see good?

♥ Do you NEVER compare yourself to others?

Hopefully, you can answer "yes" to all of these. But as so many of us have such a poor self-image, you probably answered "no" to at least one.

You also probably know that having a poor self-image is not good for you and how you view the world. But how did you get to this stage? Where does this poor self-image come from?

The Language of Love

One of the reasons why you are dismissive of yourself is because you are affected by society's beliefs and attitudes. From a very young age, you will have heard the phrase "such and such loves himself/herself," when people are trying to describe somebody who is arrogant or vain. Hearing this, your subconscious mind automatically links negative connotations to loving yourself. You would then naturally think that it was not acceptable to love yourself.

Our subconscious mind then starts to see "loving ourselves" as a negative thing. But there is a massive difference between somebody who loves herself for who she is, who accepts herself as she is, and somebody who is arrogant. Think about somebody who is arrogant or vain. How does that person talk about themselves and others? Do you like this person? Now think about somebody who actually loves herself in a good way, who is confident and happy. How does that person talk about herself and others? Do you like this person? Do you see a difference between the two?

An arrogant and vain person is stereotyped as somebody who frequently likes to look in the mirror at themselves and who loves the sound of their own voice. They are often overpowering, will monopolise the conversation and be very loud and boisterous. They want everybody to listen to them but will not even ask how the other person is feeling. They appear to everybody that they are confident and love themselves very much. But do they really?

Often this type of person is putting on a façade because deep down they are not happy with who they are. They want to have all the attention to make them feel significant, as they cannot find solace within themselves and thus try to use others to make them feel good. You will probably know people like this, and will generally dislike them, as they (in society's words) "love themselves". But remember – this is not true self-love.

When you are truly happy in yourself, you will act so differently from the person I described above. When you love yourself, you are happy, smiley and content. There seems to be a real presence about you, maybe a glow, because you are happy and your love shines through. You talk to yourself in a positive and loving way and consequently behave this way towards others. When you love yourself you do not have negative emotions towards others. You want others to be happy, which means that you will not dominate all the conversation, you will listen to them and try to understand them too.

Internal Reflections

Another major reason why you don't love yourself enough is because of the negative thoughts and limited beliefs that you dwell on, internally, every day. How much of your time and energy do you spend on negative thoughts, your inabilities, your appearance and what other people think about you?

You have over 80,000 thoughts a day and if you're anything like I used to be, then you're replaying the same negative thoughts over and over again. I used to constantly tell myself I was fat and ugly and, not surprisingly, then felt very down. If you continually play the same depressing thoughts over and over again, like a song on repeat, you're going to be totally brain-washed by your thoughts and very down on yourself. So it's time you started changing your thoughts to ones that are more encouraging and kind. Be your own best friend!

With the pictures you make in your imagination of yourself, and the way you talk to yourself, you create your own personal map of the world. If you draw your map of the world based on beliefs, that you hate yourself, you are ugly, fat and so on, then you will reflect that. You literally get what you focus on. You need your internal voice, (yes you do have an internal voice,) to help you navigate your way through the world. However, if your internal voice is negative, it won't be supporting you. *It's time you started to change this.*

Where is Your Focus?

What do you constantly focus on and say to yourself? Is it positive and encouraging or is it negative and pessimistic? Is it, "I am fat," "I wish I was more beautiful", "I wish I was more motivated,"... "I wish, I wish, I wish...." Does this actually support you and make you feel better about yourself?

If you don't talk to yourself in a positive way, you won't feel good about yourself. You must start noticing the nice things about yourself. If you find yourself saying that you can't do something, then try asking yourself, "how would I do it, if I could?" Instead of complaining about problems, come up with solutions for them. This is much more fun and is better for your own well-being. Focus on the good things in life and the good things in yourself to make you feel fabulous. It works!

So, think about what you can do with your internal voice to make you feel better. For example, when you find your internal voice is negative, does it sound stern and lower pitched? Practise, internally, talking to yourself in a cross voice for a few seconds to see how it sounds. Now change the tone of your negative voice, so you are telling yourself off in a sexy deep voice, or a high pitched cartoon voice. Try it. How does that sound? Isn't it more difficult to take your "ticking off" more seriously?

Another great method of controlling your internal voice is to turn the volume down when it's being cynical or negative. You have control over the volume, the pitch and the tone of your voice, so use it to your advantage.

Start noticing how much you currently talk to yourself internally. Is it when things are going well, or only when they are going badly? Does it open up new options or close them down? How does it leave you feeling? What can you start saying to yourself to help you to move forward instead of backwards? The language that you use to talk to yourself is critical in helping you to feel good and love yourself. Use only nice words to yourself, especially when you are looking at yourself in the mirror.

Shall I Compare Thee to a Celeb?

The negative beliefs that you hold come from so many different people and can paralyse you in life, especially the beliefs from the media. In many ways, as a young woman, you are literally trained to dislike your own body. You are constantly being bombarded with images of perfect celebrities – tall, skinny women with not an ounce of fat on their bodies. It's been estimated that a woman in the twenty first century will see more images of other women through the media in one day than her grandmother would have seen in a lifetime. This leads you to judging yourself, as I used to, as not good enough. With so many skinny celebrities being worshipped for their size and beauty, there is little wonder why we become obsessed about being skinny or that "perfect" size zero.

The media portrays size zero as cool and beautiful. But is it really? We can't all be a size zero – we simply aren't all built like that. But like many women, you probably feel pressurized to be it.

A great way of increasing your self-love is to stop having bad feelings against others. Practise having good feelings. Many of the young women that I have worked with have had problems with self-esteem and confidence because they were constantly comparing themselves to others. It was only when they realised that they must embrace who they are, that they were able to truly accept themselves.

Have you ever realised how much you compare yourself to other people? That's because society has conditioned you to do it. Think about it, in the magazines and on TV, celebrities are constantly being scrutinized in detail and compared against their peers. If the WAGS were to go on a night out, then what is the bet that there would be news stories in all the papers discussing their fashion sense and who looked the skinniest? You come to expect this. You probably compare yourself to the stars and your friends constantly. And then of course you spend money trying to look like that, which is what the advertisers and magazine editors want. Insecurity is profitable!

Until you become aware of how this is affecting you, you will not start to take control of your life and be happy with who you are.

Turnaround

This story demonstrates how the media and our internal thoughts and limited beliefs have a negative impact on our lives.

Recently, I have been working with a 20 year old client called Katy. When Katy first came to see me, she was unhappy. She told me she wanted to build her confidence, as she was worried that she was going to lose her boyfriend Robert. She said she kept accusing him of staring at other women and also continuously compared herself to other girls, as Robert made her feel inferior. She told me that when she looked in magazines or watched TV and saw glamorous skinny girls, she longed to be like them, even though she was thin already.

She felt paranoid, as she thought Robert was always looking at other women. She became so jealous, that whenever they watched TV with a pretty girl on a programme, she would have to change the channel or they would have an argument as she "knew" he fancied the girl on TV more. When they went out, it would end up in tears as she was convinced that he was staring at every girl in the restaurant, bar, club or cinema they had been to. Even when they went out with friends, they would have arguments as she believed he fancied her friends more. It was a destructive relationship, not to mention that Katy was losing her friends because of her jealous and insecure behaviour.

It sounds horrendous but maybe you have been there and often still are – jealous, insecure and compare yourself to others!

Looking at this from the outside, it could appear that Robert was not worth being with, as he had made her insecure. *The fact is nobody can make you insecure apart from yourself.* If people say awful things about you, the words might make you feel uncomfortable, but it is up to you whether you choose to believe them. You make the decision on whether to feel insecure or not. So, the real issue was about how little Katy loved herself.

Because Katy is a stunning girl, incredibly slim and fashionable, it was difficult to understand why she would compare herself to others so negatively.

Katy and Robert first met in a club and their attraction to each other was initially all about "looks". They went on a few dates and became boyfriend and girlfriend. Everything was marvellous at the beginning; they were totally hooked on each other.

This lasted for four months, until one day their relationship changed dramatically.

One summer's day, whilst Katy and Robert were sunbathing and Katy was reading a magazine, she made the fatal mistake of asking Robert what he thought of some of the celebrities in her magazine. When Robert replied that he thought Girls Aloud were "fit", Katy went mad. She could not handle the fact that he fancied other people. She shouted at him, they had an almighty row and she stormed off. He was shocked, as he had not foreseen this happening. When later he tried to explain that he fancied and loved her more than some girl band, she ignored him and carried on being defensive and angry.

That night, she told her two girl friends about the row and the fact that Robert preferred Girls Aloud to her. He hadn't actually said this but she had decided that this was so. They agreed that he was an insensitive idiot and of course started to criticize him. Unfortunately, this was feeding fuel to the fire that was burning into an unhealthy jealousy.

Katy kept replaying the images of that day in her mind and it drove her mad. Now, when she looked in the mirror, she was convinced that she was not good enough and she felt totally inadequate.

What you must remember is that, once you start to focus on something, you can make it far worse than it is by the amount of attention you give it. Katy paid far too much attention to Robert's comment that day. Subsequently, she thought he fancied every other woman he saw. Please remember you can be attracted to more than just one person in life. This does not mean that you or your partner is going to run off with another person. We all appreciate a variety of beautiful people, possessions and places in this world; this makes life exciting and is perfectly natural!

Katy's problem was that she was focusing on all of the wrong things, forgetting when Robert told her she was beautiful and that he loved her. All she could remember was that he fancied Girls Aloud. Katy now thought the only solution was to dump Robert. Yet the solution to her problem was being aware of what she was doing and changing her focus to something more empowering. Remember, *you* choose what *you* decide to focus on. To feel bad you need to delete all the good thoughts from your life. Katy was doing just this. To feel great, you have to delete the thoughts you could feel bad about. Katy was not doing this.

Katy had to learn to love herself more. She felt that she was not good enough for Robert, but she wanted his love. You need to love yourself to be able to truly love somebody else. You can't expect someone else to love you if you don't love yourself. Soon afterwards, Katy realised that she needed to love herself and not constantly compare herself to others. And this is what she did. By using the techniques and exercises at the end of the chapter, Katy has now accepted herself and loves herself.

❤ ❤

Fighting Food and Drug Addictions

You have probably heard others saying that the way to a man's heart is through his stomach. I have now changed this saying for us females! The way to a woman's heart is through her stomach, mouth and nose. So what devices do you use to fight off boredom, loneliness, anger, sadness or any other uncomfortable emotion? Do you use food, alcohol, smoking or drugs to stop yourself thinking about your emotions? Do you use these substances, as you think you will get some sort of pleasurable feeling from them? And do they make you feel better?

Those chocolate bars, biscuits, sweets and crisps might have seemed like a good idea at the time, but when you have munched your way through a quarter of your own body weight, you don't feel so great. You feel disappointed with yourself, and set off that negative voice in your head. Saying, "No wonder you're so fat. You're disgusting. Sort yourself out. You're going on a strict diet tomorrow." As you well know, this tends to end up in a vicious circle and after you have beaten yourself up, and thus lowered your self-esteem, you will again reach out for that chocolate bar to make you feel better. Can you relate to this?

Chocolate Bingeing

When I was 10 years old, I started to binge on chocolate. I will never forget the first day I did this. I was going over to my mum's house, as my parents were divorced. I found it quite strange staying with her and my step-dad, in a different environment where I didn't have my own belongings to play with. In short, I was feeling insecure.

That day, knowing that I was going to have nothing to do at my mum's house, I decided to get a magazine and some chocolate. In the sweetshop, there was an offer on Terry's Chocolate Orange, buy one get one free. I remember thinking that I would buy one for my mum and I could have some of the other one that night. In reality, it didn't quite work out that way and that night I ate both chocolate oranges in bed. And then I felt totally sick and disgusted at myself.

The seed had now been sown. I had used the chocolate as a distraction for the boredom at my mum's house. This then triggered me into doing this every time I went there. It made me feel sick but it also made me feel better in a home where I felt like I didn't belong. I associated chocolate with feeling good, because it blocked the uncomfortable feelings of boredom and loneliness.

At first, I only did this at my mum's house, but then I started to binge on chocolate whenever I was lonely or bored. If I had exam worries, boyfriend problems, friend problems, problems with feeling fat and ugly (which I consistently felt when I was a teenager), I reached out for the chocolate. But then I loathed myself the next day, and every day. My internal voice was constantly telling me that I was a pig, yet I would still carry on.

One day, my sister told me that I was getting fat. I realised from that moment onwards that I had a chocolate addiction and had to stop and so I did. Instead, I became obsessed with counting calories. Unfortunately, as my sister had told me that I was getting fat, which I was, I found it hard to stop thinking about being fat. From around 13 years onwards, I was totally and utterly obsessed with my weight. When I went out, all I thought about was who looked the thinnest, and compare myself to others. It was an absolute nightmare! Now I'm happy to say thatI don't do this any more. But, I only stopped my destructive habits and behaviours when I started treating myself with love and respect.

What distractions do you use to stop your boredom and give yourself instant pleasure? There are so many celebrities and other people that we look up to, overeating, taking drugs and drinking, to mask their problems and to feel good. Are you one of them?

Instant pleasure might feel good at the moment, but what are the consequences? Do you ever stop to think about the damage it can do to you health-wise and to your relationships with both yourself and your loved ones? What negative impact do your distractions have on your life?

Nowadays, many young women take drugs or smoke to suppress their appetite. Do you do this? Models have admitted that they take cocaine and amphetamines to deal with the pressure of remaining stick thin. Would you do something like this, something that can ultimately kill you, just to stay thin? Or are you doing it already?

If you're an overeater, binge on chocolate, starve yourself, drink too much, smoke, take drugs, shop excessively, gamble, watch TV constantly, moan and are jealous of others – *you have to STOP NOW, or you will be miserable forever.*

Take control of your life *now*. Learn how to love yourself *now*. If you want to have some chocolate, cigarettes, alcohol or drugs, remember you are associating that with pleasure, and that the pleasure will be short-lived. Is it worth it? Think of the bigger picture, the healthy, fit, happy you that is glowing – isn't that what you want? Instead of reaching for comfort distractions say to yourself, "Is this how I see my future?"

In Control

Recently, I worked with a client who had unhealthy compulsions with food. When Emma first contacted me, she was desperately unhappy and felt very out of control. She had severe problems with food and had abused it in many ways, to deal with the pressures in her life. In the past, Emma had been anorexic but was now beginning to follow a new pattern of eating excessively and bingeing because she was unhappy.

When Emma was born, she had a stroke and subsequently has a slight disability in her left arm and leg. Because of this she felt "different" to everyone else at school. She felt awkward and unhappy in herself because she did not have control over her limbs and was often treated like an outsider. Desperate to get some control in her life, she controlled what she ate, eventually becoming anorexic.

Emma became fixated with her weight whilst at school, as did most of the girls. She felt that if she didn't eat she would have more self-control. She thought that if she was skinny, she would be more popular, as her belief was that all popular girls were thin. She associated being thin with being normal and this is what she wanted to be. However, there is no such thing as normal. What is normal to you can be incredibly different to someone else.

Emma cut back on her food intake and started to see results quickly. This made her feel powerful and she carried on. Unfortunately, she took it to the extreme and became very thin, sad and withdrawn because she was not getting enough nutrition. It affected her life massively but all she could focus on was losing more weight, giving herself a feeling of control. Emma was finally admitted into hospital having battled with her dangerously low weight for two years. Luckily, she did recover but it took a long time.

When she reached a healthy weight, Emma contacted me, as she was so depressed by this much needed gain. She felt her eating was now out of control and she was disgusted with herself for putting on weight. But she finally realised that she had to stop using food in these negative ways and she was determined to overcome her eating disorders. She knew she had to change or she would never be the person she wanted and deserved to be.

During coaching sessions, we worked on Emma's self-esteem and focused on her strength of character and what she had achieved during her life. Because of that, she decided that she would take control of her life and not let her disability affect her. She started to approach the way she ate in a more sensible manner, eating healthily so that she could be full of vitality. By increasing her energy levels, she started to feel better in herself and started to take control of her life. She promised herself she would not let her disability hold her back.

Within six weeks, she turned her life around completely. She started to focus on things that would make her happy and took on new challenges such as paintballing, horse riding, abseiling and pot holing. For the first time in her life, she had a healthy relationship with food. She took care of herself and learned how to be more assertive. She also decided to join a modelling agency for women with disabilities. She totally transformed her life, just by finally accepting who she was.

I bumped into Emma the other day and I was amazed. She looked a different person. She was walking along so much more easily – as if she had more control in her leg. It was unbelievable. She told me she had decided she was going to gain more control over her limbs and was determined to strengthen them by exercising as much as she could. By focusing on what she really wanted, to be able to walk easily, she was starting to do just this. Emma was putting her control and effort into walking and not eating and this had changed her life. She really was a different person.

Emma said to me, "Six weeks ago, my aim was to be able to walk half a mile easily and that's what I'm doing! I'm so determined to walk more easily. Every day, I set myself small goals and every day I keep adding to them. It is so exciting, as I now really believe that I have the power and control to do anything in life that I want to."

And she does. If she imagines she can do something then she will.

Emma now respects and loves herself. If she has an off day now, she just tells herself that she is great and focuses on the happy elements in her life. Emma has been using positive "affirmations" and "anchors" (we will be looking at these next) every day and this has revolutionised her way of thinking.

Complete the following exercises to build up your self-esteem and love yourself wholeheartedly. I recommend that you read through these exercises every day for a week, so that they become ingrained in your subconscious mind.

❤ ❤ ❤ Self-Esteem Exercises ❤ ❤ ❤

EXERCISE ONE

Mirror Mirror on the Wall

Look in the mirror and say aloud the words that pop into your head when you look at your reflection. Write them down. Read them back to yourself aloud.

What I say about myself when I look at myself

'Ok'   'tired'   'chubby'   'teeth - not nice'.

How many are negative? Would you let a stranger say those things about you? Would you let somebody that loves you say them about you? So how come you let that inner voice talk to you like that? For you to love yourself, you need your inner voice to say more positive and encouraging words to you.

What nice things can you say about yourself? Say at least 15 positive things about yourself, even if it is that you like the colour of your eyes.

New positive words about myself

nice blue eyes, hair looks healthy, skin glowing, freckles, smile,

EXERCISE TWO

Don't Put Yourself Down

Over the course of the next week, notice every time you speak negatively about yourself and write it down. This will make you aware of how many times a day you are telling people or yourself that you are useless at things. This is a real eye opener and will automatically lead you to turn down the negative dialogue. Every time you say something negative about yourself, change your self-talk immediately to something more encouraging.

NEGATIVE COMMENTS FROM SELF	NEW POSITVE COMMENTS ABOUT SELF
DIB at work, messed it up - wont get it done.	Done amazing so for, done whats been asked. Big job, only do what I can. not 100% my responsibility.

EXERCISE THREE

How my Loved Ones see me

💜 Sit down and think of somebody who loves you.

💜 Imagine them standing in front of you and imagine yourself stepping out of your body and into the body of this person. See through their eyes all the good things that they see in you, hear through their ears all the good things that they hear and say about you, and feel the love and good feelings that they have when they are with you.

💜 Notice in detail what it is that they love about you, qualities that maybe you don't appreciate yourself.

💜 Step back into your own body and take a few moments to feel those fabulous feelings of knowing that you are loved.

💜 Take those feelings with you every day of your life and remember to recognise those qualities that others see in you.

Why I Love Myself

Over the next seven days take two minutes each morning to look in the mirror and repeat "I love you (your name), I love you (your name)" and then say the specific reasons why you love yourself. For instance, "I love you (your name) because you are so funny and you can make everybody laugh. I love the way (your name) that you do your hair and your make up (your name) is looking pretty sexy today. Say out loud "I love you" and say positive and encouraging words to yourself. Make yourself feel good and accept who you are.

EXERCISE FOUR

Imagine & You Can... Love Yourself

Visualisation time for 5 minutes every day

💜 In detail, see yourself being totally happy and loving yourself. See yourself like this in every day life. Be the director of your own movie, where you are the star.

💜 Make the movie as perfect as possible. In as much detail as you can, imagine yourself looking in the mirror and saying nice things to yourself. Hear the sounds of your own voice saying positive and reassuring comments to yourself. Imagine your inner voice telling you all the time, what a wonderful person you are. Imagine yourself really loving yourself and accepting who you are. Imagine yourself treating yourself with respect and self-love. Imagine looking after yourself and not abusing food, diets, alcohol, cigarettes or drugs. Imagine telling yourself that any negative behaviour that you have had in the past, you will not hold on to, because you now love yourself. Imagine your body movements when you walk around, knowing that you do love yourself.

♥ Once you are satisfied, associate yourself into the movie and imagine doing it for real. See what you would see if you had great self-esteem; hear what you would hear and notice how others react to you.

When you are happy with your movie, store it away in the DVD collection in your mind, knowing that you can see it, any time that you want.

EXERCISE FIVE

Affirmations

Affirmations are the key to positive thinking. Using affirmations, you can focus your mind and body for success. Affirmations are positive ideas that you can consciously choose to programme into your mind to produce your desired results. You are deliberately placing a thought in your mind on which it can act. When you give your mind the opportunity it will create what you want it to. Whatever it is you believe to be true you can develop. Through repetition you can program your mind to think positive thoughts and achieve what you desire, achieve self-love. By telling yourself that you love yourself.

I __Jane Connors__ love myself.

♥ Phrase them as if they are occurring now. For instance, if you want to be slimmer, a suitable affirmation would be "I am becoming slimmer."

♥ Don't phrase it as if it has already happened, e.g. "I am slim", because if you're not slim yet, that's what your subconscious mind will whisper to you.

♥ Write down your affirmations on the next page.

♥ Say them several times a day. This will keep them in your mind and you will start to see opportunities that you would never see otherwise.

AFFIRMATIONS

I am becoming healthier

I am starting to look after myself

I am becoming more confident

I am becoming more positive

I am becoming a better mum.

EXERCISE SIX

Getting Rid of Negative Behaviours

Write down the negative behaviours you have had in the past, such as over eating, excessive dieting, smoking etc.

♥ Negative behaviours that I had in the past

Bad Diet - Food & drink to point I become ill. ↓ self care. Allow others to miss treat me.

♥ What did I get from these negative behaviours in the past?

ill / bad mood / irratic behaviour / ↓ confidence / stopped me living a positive life. Hurt me.

❤ Instead of using these negative behaviours to hurt myself, what can I do differently?

Eat well. Ø R/bud. Good self care - books/bath / nails / yoga / nice food / dress nice.

❤ What will I gain now?

Confidence / happiness / better me / try new things / Live more instead of plodding on /

❤ How will I see myself when I look in the mirror and know that I am not indulging in these habits?

Well / glowing / Good skin & hair / ↓ eye bags / ↓ bloating / Slimmer.

❤ What will I be saying to myself and what will others be saying about me when I have stopped my negative behaviours?

You look well / good
I like your...... (clothes)

❤ What will be the positive impact on my life mentally, physically, to my relationships, in my work or school life, in my family life?

I will be happier & more Confident.
I will be a better me /friend ect.
excel more.

❤ What do I need to remember and do, to stop myself going back to negative behaviours, so that I can really show that I love myself?

Remember that I need to ♡ myself by looking after me - (R) how shitty I feel when I dont.

EXERCISE SEVEN

Special Gifts

Reflect on your special gifts. What are they? Maybe you have the gift of being able to talk for England? Or maybe you have the gift of style and being able to put an outfit together simplistically. Or maybe you have the gift of enjoying exercise? Or maybe you have the gift of being a fantastic friend because you are loyal and kind and a good listener. You will have hundreds of fantastic gifts but just think of 15 for now.

How could you use them more to enrich your life?

MY FANTASTIC GIFTS	HOW TO USE THEM MORE
Running	Join club.
Kind / caring	New job opportunities
Good cook	Cook more / Dinner Party.

EXERCISE EIGHT

Anchoring Yourself into a Positive State

Anything that consistently happens to you whilst you are in an extremely emotional state becomes associated with that state. This is known as 'anchoring'. As an example, can you think of a particular song, that whenever you hear it, reminds you of a person that you used to be in a relationship with? The reason for this is because the song was probably being played in the background at the peak of this extremely emotional state. A link was then formed in your mind and body so that each time you hear that song your memory is filled with the intense feelings of that occasion once again. People are always anchoring. We constantly associate and create meaning, frequently at a subconscious level, out of experiences that are occurring around us. Understanding anchoring is the secret. This will enable you to take conscious control and to anchor good feelings, to put you into a positive state of mind, so that when you are feeling a little unhappy you can alter your emotions immediately to a more positive state. You can completely change your life by mastering this skill.

How to Create Positive Anchors

💗 To get yourself into an excited state you need to think about a time when you were excited.

💗 Breathe how you would breathe when you are excited, smile the way you smile, move the way that you move, say the things or make the sounds when you are really excited and happy.

💗 Whilst you are in this state, do something original over and over again so that you have created an anchor. Linking an anchor to this state is key to it being powerful. This anchor could be tapping your foot and shouting "yes" each time you feel that you are at the peak of your state. If you keep repeating it and adding more emotional intensity, this will make your anchor far more powerful.

💗 Then test the anchor. Relax. Shift your focus onto something else. After a minute, use the anchor, tapping your foot and shouting "Yes!" You should feel your body going right back into that peak state.

💗 Build yourself a positive anchor now, so you are able to use this at a time when you might otherwise feel low. Create a switch button in your mind, so you can easily switch on those good vibes and loving feelings towards yourself and others.

Love Myself Self-Coaching

To feel better about yourself, use this self-coaching session and carry out the actions to improve your self-love. Allow yourself 30-45 minutes to do this.

G is for Goal

(On a scale of 1-10, where 1 is "not at all" and 10 is "completely happy")

💜 How much do I love myself? ___7___

💜 What do I need to do to make it a 10?

dress nicer / eat better / mae self care.

💜 Think about loving and respecting yourself and take yourself forward to a point in time where you love yourself completely and are totally happy and accepting of yourself. What do you notice that shows that you love yourself? How do you know this has happened?

Happy, Glowing, relaxed As I am a (pr) $ have looked after myself.

💜 What are you hearing that tells you that you love yourself?

I am worth the effort / I am important $ need to be no.1.

💜 How are you feeling at this point in the future?

Happy, motivated, calm, embracing Life.

💜 What are you saying to yourself?

You can do this - You are doing it - keep going - Fab things are happening

❤ How will you know that you love yourself? Is there a measurement you can use?

My mood/ how much i look after
myself.

R is for Reality

❤ What is going on right now that tells you that you don't love yourself?

❤ What have you done to improve things?

❤ What were the obstacles you encountered in doing these things?

❤ What possible barriers are in your way that prevent you from moving forward?

❤ What do you need to do, to help you to love yourself?

_____

_____

_____

❤ Are there any resources that might help you to love yourself more?

_____

_____

_____

O is for Options

Now that we have clarified how we love ourselves and what has happened in the past, let's consider the options available to you to move forward.

❤ What could you do to move yourself just one step forward now?

_____

_____

_____

❤ Go wild and write down as many ways that you can think of to love yourself more.

_____

_____

_____

_____

_____

❤ If you could devote all your time to loving yourself, what would you do then?

_____

_____

_____

_____

❤ If you went to your guardian angel for help to love yourself more, what might she suggest?

_____

_____

_____

❤ What could you do if money was unlimited, to love yourself more?

_____

_____

_____

❤ If you secretly know what you should do first, what would it be?

_____

_____

_____

_____

❤ Choose one of the options that you think would be right for you to do now. Circle it. But, will it move you forward? If not choose something else.

❤ How will this option make you love yourself more?

_____

_____

_____

_____

W is for Will

❤ What will you do? List the actions so that you start to love yourself more?

_____

_____

_____

_____

♥ How will these actions allow you to love yourself more?

_____

_____

_____

♥ When are you going to take these actions?

_____

_____

_____

♥ Should anybody else be involved in this list of actions?

_____

_____

_____

♥ What do you want this person, or these people to do?

_____

_____

_____

_____

♥ When will you tell them?

_____

_____

_____

♥ Who else should know that you are doing these things?

_____

_____

_____

_____

🖤 When will you tell them?

_____

_____

_____

_____

🖤 Whatever your first step is, can you think of any obstacle that might stop you from doing it?

_____

_____

_____

_____

🖤 How likely is it to stop you? If likely, what can you do to make your first step more achievable?

_____

_____

_____

_____

🖤 What will you do to prevent it from stopping you?

_____

_____

_____

_____

🖤 Is there anything else you need to consider before you begin?

_____

_____

_____

_____

💜 On a scale of 1-10 where 10 is "I am totally committed to loving myself and taking action", where are you?

_____

_____

_____

_____

💜 If you are not a 10 – what do you need to do to make it a 10?

_____

_____

_____

_____

Chapter Three

Be Confident in all Situations

To be confident or not to be confident, that is the question.

Confident: to have a feeling of certainty about yourself; to be self-assured, positive, and self-reliant.

In this Chapter you will:

- Speak to yourself positively to feel confident
- Use the right body language to feel confident
- Learn how to dress confidently
- Be confident in all situations

Practise Becoming Confident

Are you aware that you can be supremely confident in some situations and yet at other times you can feel really embarrassed, clam up and want to hide away from the world? Wouldn't it be amazing if you could change this and be confident all the time? After you have absorbed this chapter you will know how to do just this.

So many of my friends and clients have said to me in the past "I am not confident!" When I ask them if they are sure about that, they assertively declare, "Of course I am." The problem is that they don't lack confidence, but are certain about the wrong things. In fact, they are adamant that they have no confidence. Many of us believe that we are not confident in certain situations, ranging from job interviews, presentations, meeting new people and so on. Because we believe that we are not confident, we put ourselves in a negative state before the event and feel scared when we come to it.

You can be confident in any situation, you just need to practise. It really is as simple as that. We all feel nervous and scared sometimes throughout our lives. That is just part of being human. Nevertheless, it is important to control this fear or else it will stop you from doing the things in life that you want. Start seeing yourself being confident in all situations, from now on.

So what exactly does being confident mean to you? When you have said to yourself in the past "I wish I was more confident when meeting new people," or "I wish I was confident all the time" what sort of images come up in your mind? How do you picture yourself? Are you meek and mild, fading away into the background? Seeing yourself like that *will not* get you to where you want to be. So, now ask yourself a more empowering question: how do you *want* to see yourself?

The first major secret to being confident is imagining yourself being confident and looking like you are. If you look confident, then you will start to feel confident.

Outward Appearance

The way you use your body and face determines how people perceive you and how confident you feel. If you are unable to keep still and your eye contact is shifting continuously, then you will appear and feel uneasy. If your posture is habitually defensive, then people will not feel comfortable around you. Your body language affects how you feel. By identifying your body language and consciously adopting an alternative behaviour, you can increase your confidence levels.

Think of someone who is really confident. What is their body language like and how do they move? Do they stand tall or do they slump? Do they stand comfortably with their hands and arms relaxed at their sides or do they fidget with objects and personal belongings to channel their tension? Do they smile and have good eye contact with others or do they look to the floor?

Confident people will project their self assurance by how they hold themselves and how they act around others. A confident person will stand tall, shoulders back, chest lifted and stomach pulled in, so that their posture is upright. A confident person looks others in the eye and maintains good eye contact. They will be happy in their own skin. When you are confident, you walk into a room with presence; you might stride with style or walk slowly at ease. Either way, you are happy to strut your stuff.

The following signals often suggest what is seen to be positive (confident behaviour) or negative (nervous behaviour) and can subconsciously affect how you feel about yourself.

Positive Signals

- Not folding your arms in front of your chest and stomach so that you are open and welcoming to others.
- Showing open palms of your hands, as this suggests that you are not hiding anything.
- Standing comfortably with an upright posture and hands and arms relaxed, at your side. This helps to show that there are no boundaries.
- Leaning closer, indicating interest in others.
- Sitting asymmetrically, demonstrating confidence in taking space.
- Angling your body and crossing your legs in the direction of the person that you most like or want to establish rapport with.
- Mirroring a person's body language to gain rapport and trust with them.
- Smiling at others and having good eye contact.

Negative Signals

- Playing with objects or personal belongings, such as a handbag, rings, pencils, mobile phone.
- Mannerisms, such as nail biting, finger and foot tapping, playing with hair, adjusting clothing, chewing gum, smoking.
- Waving your fist, pointing at people and repetitive nervous gestures.
- Touching the face – this is associated with self doubt, guilt and irritation.
- Touching the nose – this is often seen as an indication of lying.
- Touching the eyes – this is often taken to mean that you don't like what you're seeing and don't want to see it any more.
- Touching the ears – this can suggest you don't like what you're hearing.
- Touching the chin and mouth – this often suggests that you have some doubt; you are reluctant to speak or do not agree with what is being said.

Read through both the positive and negative signals again and think about when you have used any of these. What were you feeling at the time when you did these? What do you need to do with your body language to make you appear and feel more confident?

Your body language not only plays a huge role in your feeling self assured, but so do your clothes. Have you ever, while getting ready to go out, felt so uncomfortable in your outfit that you decided to stay in? I know I have! The way we look is crucial to how we feel and plays a vital part in our confidence.

Unfortunately, appearance is important as we judge others by the way that they look. First impressions count!

Picture this: you walk into a party and spot two guys sitting down near the bar. One of the guys is sitting fairly upright, dressed in nice jeans, a pair of clean trainers and a fitted T-shirt. He has a bit of a David Beckham hair cut and look. He suddenly catches your eye and smiles at you. The other guy is slumped in his chair. He is wearing scruffy jeans, dirty trainers and a T-shirt that is too big for him giving him no body shape. He has greasy hair, his eyes are hidden by his fringe and he is looking pretty miserable and stand-offish. Which one would you rather talk to?

The phrase "a picture paints a thousand words" is very true. The picture or image that we see of somebody will often affect our behaviour towards them. We naturally gravitate towards people who are happy and smiley and are drawn towards those that have a similar style to our own.

Every day, you have to think about your attire and whether it will be suitable for what you are doing. You have all sorts of clothes made for different functions. You would not wear an outfit for a job interview on your girly night out, and you would not wear your school uniform or work clothes to the gym.

What we wear is about being functional, portraying the right image and making us feel confident. Have you ever been to a party and thought it was going to be a dressy affair, only to find that all your friends are wearing jeans? This can make you feel really self-conscious as you look different to your friends and you don't feel like part of the group. Finding out what others are wearing can help to stop you feeling uneasy.

We all use clothes to enhance our figures and our self-confidence. Use your wardrobe to your advantage and dress to impress. Feel good about yourself before you have stepped out the door!

Dress to Feel Fabulous

💜 If you are going to a party, an interview, a wedding, a posh event or a night out with the girls, then find out what the attire is. This will stop you turning up to an event and feeling out of place, embarrassed and uncomfortable.

💜 If you are going out later and you are going to be in a rush, then plan your outfit ahead, so that you are not stressing about it, an hour beforehand.

💜 Whether you're a jeans and trainers girl, or love your pencil skirts and killer heels, always try to look your best, as this will make you feel better and be more confident.

💜 Wear clothes that show off your figure. If you have long legs and like to show them off, then do just that. Wear clothes that you are comfortable in, but also make you feel superbly confident. There is nothing worse than seeing girls who obviously feel uncomfortable in their "new" dress, as they are constantly tugging at it and putting their hands in front of their stomach or boobs to hide themselves. Only wear outfits that make you feel good and don't feel pressurised by your friends on a girly night out to wear a particular dress, if you don't feel comfortable in it.

💜 Wear what makes you feel good. If you do find it hard knowing what looks good on you, spend some time in the shops trying on clothes and seeing how you look and how they make you feel. Go with your gut feeling. It is usually right! There are tons of books by Trinny and Susanna and other stylists that can help you.

💜 Spend time on getting your hair right – it is one of the first things that we notice about somebody. We often feel like a million dollars when we've just had our hair cut or coloured, so pay attention to your hairstyle.

💜 Wear make-up that suits you and don't go overboard like a drag queen. Blusher, mascara and lipstick are great in the day. At night, maybe add some foundation and eye shadow to give you a different look. If you don't know what suits you, then invest in a make up or a colours lesson to help you with your image. A few years ago, I went to a "House of Colour" specialist to have a make up lesson. She gave me some great tips on what did and didn't suit me.

💜 A great bag and shoes can often make your outfit and help you feel good about yourself.

💜 A smile always makes others feel at ease.

Self-Talk

Your self-talk affects how you feel every minute of the day. If you don't feel confident, then you must have negative self-talk which is making you paranoid and fearful.

It is impossible to *feel* confident and have negative self-talk. You can *act* confident and have negative self-talk, but to be properly confident you need to be in full control of your own mind. Remember a time when you have been nervous, such as meeting new people. What unhelpful words did you say to yourself, to feel even more worried?

Being Positive

I recently worked with a girl called Carly who was *amazing* at scaring herself before any new situation. Carly had just joined an impressive Public Relations firm in London. One of her roles as a PR Assistant was to go to client functions and network with strangers. Carly felt she had little confidence and was incredibly apprehensive about how she was going to carry out her job. In our session, we worked on her demons (self-talk) so she could do her job well. Here is an extract of our conversation:

Carly: I really want to be confident so that I am able to network and socialise with my clients and their customers and feel good about myself but I am scared witless. I don't know why I took this job on, I must have been mad.

*Davinia: What **did** make you take this job?*

Carly: I love doing all the creative stuff in PR, the copy writing and so on. That was the main reason why I went for the job. I sort of hoped that I wouldn't have to do too much networking in big groups, but I was definitely kidding myself there. Everything I do is with big groups.

Davinia: You said that you hoped you wouldn't have to network in big groups? What do you mean by that?

Carly: Well, I don't like going to a party or a new situation where there are lots of people I don't know. I am fine if there are only a few, but when there are lots of people I feel nervous and lose all my confidence.

Davinia: I am hearing you say that you do feel confident in some situations, such as when there are fewer people around, is that right?

Carly: Yes!

Davinia: Can you explain the difference to me?

Carly: I have been in many situations with just a few people and so I'm comfortable with this. But when there are lots of people it scares me, as I don't know what to say and I find that I question myself.

(This was the breakthrough stage – Carly is questioning herself in certain situations and therefore this is where her negative self-talk is making her feel insecure.)

Davinia: So what do you say when you are questioning yourself?

(Carly then told me about all the different running commentaries in her head.)

Carly: "I don't know anybody at this event and there are so many people. It's going to be a nightmare. I've been dreading this all week. I want to go home now. Pull yourself together! It will be fine! You can do it! You look lovely and everything is fine.

But why am I so fat? Why do my trousers feel so tight? Ssh! Stop being so negative. Right, enough is enough, I need to start mingling. But I don't know anybody. OK just be brave, go and talk to somebody. You can do it. Right... who am I going to speak to first? Nobody is on their own, so I'll have to go and approach a group of people. Oh my god, what the hell am I going to say? This is so embarrassing. Maybe I should just hide in the loo? No don't be so silly, you can do this. You can talk to a few people and if it is really awful you can pretend you are ill in an hour or so and just go home...

Ok, none of them look that friendly and I'm sure that group of people keep staring at me. Why are they laughing? Are they laughing at me? They are, aren't they? They think I'm fat and my clothes look crap. They know I don't fit in. I knew I shouldn't have worn these shoes. Oh my god, why do I always feel like this? I wish I had more confidence. I can't bear it. I just want to hide. I feel horrible and look horrible."

Having finished sharing her negative self-talk with me, Carly sat in absolute silence, stunned by the stupidity of it. She had never consciously thought about how damaging her self-talk was. This self-realisation for Carly was incredibly powerful and was the turning point for her transformation. Try this yourself – say your negative self-talk out loud or, even better, write it down in a speech like Carly's. Do you see how ridiculous it looks?

I then asked Carly to tell me what she tells herself going into situations where she feels confident. She said, "I tell myself that I'm going to have fun and everybody will like me as I'm a nice person. I tell myself I look good and feel good and everything will be great." It was amazing how different her self-talk was for comfortable situations.

By highlighting these differences, Carly was able to move forward. She started using the same positive words when going to networking events and she felt good. In fact, she is now fantastic at networking and very confident.

Did Carly's negative self-talk sound like the sort of conversation that you have had in your head, unsupportive and destructive? Often, when we are panicking about something and not feeling comfortable in a situation, our mind will jump from one thing to another and we can hallucinate silly things such as "everybody is laughing at me". It is impossible to feel and be confident when you have negative chatter taking place in your head.

Like Carly, think about times when you feel confident and think about what you say to yourself. Use these same words as encouragement when you are going into new situations. Practise saying positive things to yourself. Be aware of your self-talk and if it is negative, change it instantly. If you tell yourself before you go somewhere that it is going to be an awful night, then it will be. Your mind has been made up before you even get there. It is far better to say positive things to get you in the right frame of mind.

❤ ❤

Tell yourself that you are confident; that you are wonderful and you can do anything that you want to do. Make sure when you are speaking to yourself that not only are your words but also your tone of voice is encouraging. You can say positive words to yourself such as "you are fabulous" but if you say them in a voice that is full of sarcasm you won't believe it. Your voice should not sound scornful but motivating and upbeat.

Pictures in your Mind

The last ingredient to being totally confident is about what you are picturing in your mind. Imagine going to a party. Picture yourself in the room with nobody to talk to, looking miserable, lonely and in a disastrous outfit. This will not inspire you to go to the party and this scenario would make you feel totally lacking in confidence.

On the other hand, if you imagine yourself talking to lots of people, laughing, dancing with your new friends and looking really hot in your outfit, then you will feel excited about going to the party. What we see in our minds is crucial to our success and confidence. You need to imagine the party or the situation that you are going to encounter to be fun and exciting. You need to see yourself having a good time with the other people there. If you imagine a disastrous day ahead with everything going severely wrong, then it inevitably will be. If you set your day up to be great and you see yourself as happy, confident and enjoying the day, then you are pretty much guaranteed to experience this.

So many people think that confidence is something that you either have or you haven't. But in fact, you decide at any given moment whether you are going to be confident in a situation by what you are focusing on. If you focus on good images, have upbeat self-talk, positive body language while you dress to impress, you will not fail to be confident in any situation.

EXERCISE ONE

Confidence Anchor

Get yourself into a confident state by first thinking about a time when you felt really confident.

- Breathe how you would breathe when you are confident, smile the way you smile, move the way that you move, say the things or make the sounds when you are really confident.

- While you are in this confident state, do something unique over and over again, so that you have created an anchor. Linking a trigger to this state is the key to it being powerful. This anchor could be clapping your hands and saying repeatedly "I am confident." If you keep repeating it and adding more emotional intensity, this will make your anchor far more powerful.

❤ Then test the anchor. Relax. Change your focus to something else. After a minute, use the anchor, clapping your hands and saying "I am confident." You should feel your body going right back into that peak state.

EXERCISE TWO

Confident Self-Talk

Go through times when you have felt really confident in yourself. Remember what you said and write down all the things that you have said and would need to say to make yourself feel good in all situations.

What I need to say to feel confident:

_____

_____

_____

_____

_____

_____

Practise Confident Physiology

Over the next week, each day practise standing in front of your mirror in a confident manner. Think about your posture and what you need to do to look confident. Use your confidence anchor and keep reinforcing to yourself how wonderful you are and how confident you are and how you can do whatever you want.

EXERCISE THREE

Clothes for Confidence

Go through your wardrobe and get rid of any items you don't feel good in, even if they were impulse purchases and you have never worn them. Sell them on eBay and make some money or give them to charity. Go through clothes that you can wear for different occasions. Have outfits at the ready for posh events, girly nights out, casual days, interviews and so on. What do you need to do to your wardrobe to make yourself feel more confident? Write down what you need to do and take action.

_____

_____

_____

_____

_____

_____

_____

_____

_____

EXERCISE FOUR

Hair and Make Up

Go through your make up and decide whether it is right. Throw away any you don't use. Should you book a make up lesson? Go to your hairdresser's for a revamp and ask for advice.

EXERCISE FIVE

Daily Exercise

Take some form of exercise, every day. When you exercise, your body releases the chemical endorphins into your blood stream which instantly makes you feel good in yourself and will increase your confidence. Write down in your diary what exercise you have done that day.

EXERCISE SIX

Laugh

Laugh for twenty minutes a day, minimum. Laughter is fantastic for lifting our spirits and can improve our overall mood and wellbeing dramatically. Like exercise, it produces endorphins to make the body feel good.

EXERCISE SEVEN

Imagine & You Can... Be Confident

Visualisation time for 5 minutes every day

❤ See yourself in detail being incredibly confident. See yourself like this in every day life. Be the director of your own movie, where you are the star.

❤ Make the movie as perfect as possible. Imagine yourself being confident and content in all situations of your life. Imagine that every situation runs to plan as you are confident and at ease. See how you walk when you are confident. See how comfortable you feel in what you are wearing and how fabulous you look because you are smiling. See how you act with others that are around you, now that you are more confident. See the body language and hand gestures that you use when you are confident.

❤ Hear what you say to yourself in this assertive and cool headed state. Hear what others say about you, when you are in this positive manner.

❤ Feel how it feels, when you feel certain about yourself.

❤ Once you are satisfied, see yourself in your movie and imagine doing it for real. See what you will see when you are confident, hear what you will hear and notice how others react to you.

When you are happy with your movie, store it away in the DVD collection in your mind, knowing that you can see it any time that you want.

Self Coaching for Confidence

This coaching session is to enable you to be more confident in all situations.

G is for Goal

(On a scale of 1-10, where 1 is "not at all" and 10 is "completely happy")

❤ How would you rate your main level of confidence?_____

❤ What would make it a 10?

_____

_____

_____

💜 Think about being confident and take yourself forward to a point in time when you are totally confident in yourself. What do you notice that shows you that you are totally confident? How do you know that this has happened?

_____

_____

💜 What are you doing that shows you that you are confident? Make a quick note.

_____

_____

_____

💜 What are you hearing that tells you that you are confident?

_____

_____

💜 How are you feeling at this point in the future?

_____

_____

💜 What are you saying to yourself?

_____

_____

R is for Reality

💜 What is going on right now that tells you that you are not always confident?

_____

_____

💜 What have you done so far to improve things?

_____

_____

_____

♥ What were the obstacles you met in doing these things?

_____

_____

♥ What do you need to do to help you to be more confident?

_____

_____

♥ Are there any resources that might help you to be more confident?

_____

_____

O is for Options

♥ Now we are going to explore the sort of actions that you can take to get you to be totally confident in yourself.

♥ What could you do to move yourself one step forward now?

_____

_____

♥ Write down as many ways that you can think of, to make yourself more confident.

_____

_____

♥ What else could you do, if you didn't have to be answerable to anybody?

_____

_____

♥ If you could devote all your time to making yourself confident, what would you do then?

_____

_____

_____

💜 If you went to your guardian angel for help to be confident, what would she suggest?

_____

_____

💜 What could you do to be more confident, if money was unlimited?

_____

_____

💜 If you secretly know what you should do first, what would it be?

_____

_____

💜 Choose one of the options above that you think would be right for you to do now and circle it. If you do the one thing that you have chosen, will it move you forward? If not choose something else.

💜 How will this option make you more confident?

_____

_____

W is for Will

💜 What are you going to do?

_____

_____

💜 How will these actions allow you to be more confident?

_____

_____

💜 When are you going to take these actions? What time scales?

_____

_____

❤ How long do you think it will take you?

_____

_____

❤ Should anybody else be involved in this list of actions?

_____

_____

❤ What do you want this person, or these people to do?

_____

_____

❤ When will you tell them?

_____

_____

❤ Who else should know that you are doing these things?

_____

_____

❤ When will you tell them?

_____

_____

❤ Whatever your first step is, can you think of any obstacle that might stop you from doing it?

_____

_____

❤ How likely is it to stop you? If likely, what can you do to make your first step more achievable?

_____

_____

🖤 How will you overcome this obstacle?

_____

_____

🖤 What will you do to stop it from stopping you?

_____

_____

🖤 Is there anything else you need to consider before you begin?

_____

_____

_____

🖤 On a scale of 1-10 where 10 is "I am totally committed to being confident and taking action," where are you?

🖤 If you are not a 10 – what do you need to do to make it a 10?

_____

_____

_____

Chapter Four

Be Motivated & Achieve
Your Dreams

*To be motivated, or not to be motivated
that is the question.*

*Motivate: to stimulate interest or to prompt,
drive, move, inspire, stimulate, influence
or encourage.*

In this Chapter you will:

💜 Understand what motivates you

💜 Motivate yourself through words to take action

💜 Find out when you are at your best

💜 Find out what you want from life

Step into Action

Wouldn't it be amazing if you could motivate yourself to do the things you don't want to do, but need to do, in order to make your dreams happen? What an amazing difference this would make to your life. What if I shared some strategies with you to stop you from procrastinating and help you to become more motivated? Imagine how wonderful it would be if by the end of this chapter you are motivated to make your dreams into a reality. Excited? You should be!

Too many people in life hesitate. They wait and wait, hoping that something wonderful will come along for them. But unfortunately, life doesn't work like that. If you keep waiting and never take action, then you simply won't get what you want. Do not fall into the "manana" trap, by putting something off until tomorrow, or hoping it will just happen for you. If you want something in life, then take action. Have the tenacious conviction that you can make things happen. Be motivated and determined, in both your body and mind. Believe you will achieve what you want.

What are you like when you are motivated? Think about it. When you are motivated you communicate to people with enthusiasm. You are upbeat and excited. You will talk about your future and certainly not dwell on the past. You are positive and you expect to succeed. You have an abundance of energy. You are contagious and are excited about your life and projects.

So now, think back to a time when you were incredibly motivated and determined. This can be to do with anything: going out with your friends, looking for a new job, playing a sport, taking on a new health regime or learning a new skill. What did you do that showed others that you were motivated? How did you speak when you were motivated? How did it feel when you were motivated? And what sort of things were you saying to yourself at this time?

By remembering that experience, did you manage to get yourself motivated and excited again? If not, then try again to remember exactly what you did when you were motivated. Once you have remembered how this felt, you will realise that you can access this motivated state *at any time*. By remembering exactly how you felt, what you were saying to yourself, what you looked like and how you sounded, you can use this knowledge to put yourself into a motivated state. *Remember, your mind has encoded all these memories and can access these feelings, whenever you want them.*

Motivating Words

The words you use can dramatically change how you feel. We all use different words to inspire us to take action. Motivational speakers and coaches use very colourful and intense language to capture their audience's attention and create enthusiasm. All great speakers, such as John F Kennedy and Martin Luther King, moved us by the use of their words. We forget that every single day we influence ourselves through the words we use, whether positive or negative. *You can instantly change how you feel by the words you use to describe your experiences to yourself.*

For many people the words "I should" are very uninspiring. Yet they often use this phrase to try to motivate themselves to do something. "I *should* go to the gym, I *should* eat brussel sprouts, I *should* drink water, I *should* be good," and so on. These words rarely inspire us to do these things, because we associate "I should" with things that we *ought* to do, but don't necessarily *want* to do.

Paradoxically then, the phrase "I shouldn't" is a trigger for us to *do* something, even though we shouldn't. This is because our nervous system has been conditioned to associate the phrase "I shouldn't" with instant pleasure.

How many times have you said "I *shouldn't* eat that chocolate, I *shouldn't* buy that dress, I *shouldn't* go out tonight, I *shouldn't* ring him, I *shouldn't* have another drink" and then do the exact opposite? The words we use trigger our behaviours. When you know which words motivate you to carry out the right action, it makes tasks a lot easier to complete.

Changing Your Internal Self-Talk

I recently worked with a girl called Tracy, who really wanted to lose weight and start exercising but simply couldn't motivate herself to start. Here's an extract from one of our conversations, which will show you how changing your internal self-talk will motivate you to take the action you want:

Tracy: *I want to be more motivated so that I'll go to the gym. I want to lose weight, tone up and feel good about myself again. I know that by going to the gym that this will happen but I'm still not motivated to do it.*

Davinia: *OK! That sounds like a lot of fabulous reasons for going to the gym. By working out you'll definitely benefit in all those ways. So what's stopping you?*

Tracy: *I don't know. I know I should go but I just feel tired and don't feel like going to the gym after a long day at work. It seems like too much effort.*

Davinia: *So how do you want to feel?*

Tracy: *I want to feel excited about going and to be inspired.*

Davinia: *You said earlier that you should go. Who is telling you that you should go? If someone told me that I should do something then I wouldn't feel excited about doing it.*

Tracy: Well nobody has told me that I should go, apart from myself, because I want to feel good about myself again.

Davinia: OK! So what do you have to say to yourself to make you feel good about something that you want to do?

Tracy: (She pauses for a minute) I'm not sure.

Davinia: What do you really love doing?

Tracy: I love going out with my friends.

Davinia: And what do you say to yourself to make you want to go out with your friends?

Tracy: I don't really, I just think, I can't wait to go out with my friends. I imagine having fun with them and think about what a good time we're going to have, chatting and dancing the night away.

*Davinia: So, you're saying to yourself, I **can't wait** to go out with my friends. Instead of saying "I should go to the gym," why not say, "I can't wait to go to the gym." How does that make you feel?*

Tracy: Yes, a bit better.

Davinia: Now imagine yourself going to the gym and having a good time. Don't think about it as a chore. Just think when you are on the treadmill, you can listen to the music that you love on your iPod. Or, you can go to an aerobics class where you're exercising and working out to music, which is similar to dancing. Could you imagine it being fun then?

Tracy: Yes, that sounds like more fun.

Davinia: OK! Now imagine yourself chatting to other people you've met at the gym. Does that make it seem more appealing?

Tracy: Ooh yes it does! I think I've been looking at it the wrong way. I love my music and I love chatting to people and I can experience both of these at the gym. Yes! I think that will do it.

Davinia: So what are you going to say to yourself now when you want to go the gym?

Tracy: I can't wait to go to the gym, it will be great fun!

Initially, Tracy was totally uninspired by the gym because of the language she was using and the negative thoughts that she was having about going. By applying the thoughts and language that Tracy used when she was positive and motivated, we were able to create the same feelings for the gym and thus motivate her.

💜 💜

What Words Work for You?

What words fire you up? Go through the list below and see which words encourage you to take action and make you feel motivated. Think of something that you want to do, but you are finding hard to do – for example, going to the gym, and then try out the following words to see if any of them push you more towards the action that you want to take.

I should go the gym, I shouldn't go to the gym, I have to go to the gym…. And so on.

I should…

I shouldn't…

I have to…

I must…

I ought to…

I need to…

I want to…

I am going to…

I can't wait to…

Which words made you feel more motivated about taking action? Now, think back to that time when you were highly motivated and remember the words that you used to get yourself stimulated. By knowing what words drive you forward, you have more ammunition to get you into the motivated state that you want.

Understanding what Motivates You

We all motivate ourselves by having a vision. Your vision might not necessarily be a clear image, but you will have an idea of what you want or don't want. You will know how you want to feel or don't want to feel. You will know what you want others to say or not say about what you have done. By imagining a fantastic outcome or visualising the worst scenario that forces you to take action, you are able to motivate yourself.

Imagine that you want to lose weight, but are finding it hard to motivate yourself. Your friend, who has successfully lost weight, tells you that she did it by visualising herself being slim. She tells you that she kept seeing herself as a size 10 and because this was something that she wanted so much, she was motivated to go to the gym and eat healthily. She imagined everybody saying how great she looked and also imagined how great she would feel because she had lost the weight. Her motivational strategy was, in NLP terms, "a moving towards" strategy. She was motivated by imagining how she wanted to be, and this inspired her to move in this direction.

Spurred on by your friend's success, you try out her motivational strategy. You do exactly what she does, visualise yourself being slim, imagine how it will feel and hear the compliments that friends and family will say to you. But it doesn't seem to be working. After a week, you feel frustrated and angry and blame yourself for not feeling how your friend did. But it could be that this strategy is wrong for you.

Some people are motivated instead by a "moving away" strategy. You imagine something being so horrendous that you move away from this happening. This means, in the example of losing weight, you need to visualise yourself being so obese that it prompts you to get down to the gym quick. Imagine yourself feeling unattractive, disgusting and miserable which spurs you to take action. Imagine hearing people saying such rude remarks about your thighs and stomach that you take immediate action.

Knowing which of these is your motivational strategy will allow you to use your imagination in the right way to drive you forwards. So which strategy do you use?

Highly motivated people are great at visualising the outcome that they want. Using pleasure and pain to motivate you is crucial to your success. When I first started writing my book, I had so many ideas that I wondered how I would capture these in words to convey my message. Only when I visualised the end result did I became inspired to write my book. In my "mind's eye" I saw the book. I imagined what I would put into my book to help make a difference to my readers. I constantly reminded myself of how it would help benefit my readers' lives. My motivation for writing this book was not only to enable me to grow as a person but to help others grow. By creating a compelling outcome, I used this pleasure to keep me motivated.

Chunks

I find the "little and often" approach usually works for me. Take small steps, so that you don't feel overwhelmed. For instance, if you want to take up running and have never run before and start running flat out for a mile, what do you think will happen? You will probably not finish the mile and feel disheartened. Or you will exhaust yourself so much that you put yourself off running for life because it was so difficult. Or worse still, you injure yourself. In essence, you have taken yourself way out of your comfort zone and your brain will resist, causing you to lack motivation. But if you started off very slowly, walked one block one day, two the next day and jogged a bit on the third day, your brain won't notice that you are sneaking out of the familiar into action, until you have already begun to benefit from the momentum of change. Once you have started to take action, the momentum increases.

To succeed at anything without feeling overwhelmed, take a variety of actions and group them together, so that you can accomplish your outcome. In our minds, we group items of information into larger and smaller units, for example breaking down a large project into smaller tasks. This is known as chunking. Chunking enables you to organise your thinking. When we remember phone numbers, we cluster the digits into chunks. Chunking also allows you to become more efficient at categorising information.

If you have a big goal but no clear pathway, you will probably lack the motivation to go for it. In fact, you may feel stressed and give up. It is important that you give yourself manageable chunks, to get you to your final destination. Keep reminding yourself of the end goal and create a master plan. Have a picture, or create a vision board, so that you create the motivation and good feelings from within. This is exactly what I did with my book. I created myself a vision board, of what I wanted my book to look like, to remind me of the end result. Then I focused on one chapter at a time. This helped massively and this is what most people do, when they want to succeed in a big project. Chunk it down into small steps and keep your eye on the prize.

What Drives You?

Knowing your core values will help you get the life that you want.

So what exactly are values? Values are personal rules you live your life by. They are symbolic in what you believe is important in your life, have an impact on how you lead your life, and also how you respond to different situations. They are closely linked to your identity and help you with your direction and motivation in accomplishing projects and tasks. Our values are the things that we all need to move towards. They even determine what you will move away from. From what you wear and what you drive to where you live, who your friends are, who you marry (if you marry), from what you choose to do for a living; the impact of your values is endless.

It is important that you understand your core values. If you don't fulfil them, you will feel disappointed and empty. Your goals and dreams are based on your values. Let me help you understand this with an example.

Imagine that your most important value is to be happy. Your current job is making you incredibly unhappy, so you give in your notice. Your boss is very upset, as she thinks you are excellent at your job and doesn't want to lose you. She tells you that she will pay whatever it takes to keep you there. But can money buy you happiness? You might decide to stay because of another £2,000 in your pay packet. Yet, two months down the line the excitement of the extra money wears off. Do you feel dissatisfied and unfulfilled again?

Now you know that when you go for a job, money is not the most important value. Your core values are happiness and fulfilment. Knowing this, at your next job interview, ask the employer questions to help you to see if you will be happy there. For instance, if you knew that you liked an hour lunch break, to finish at 5pm to go to the gym, to never work at weekends, to only work with young people, none of which would be an option in your new job, then you would know not to take it.

By eliciting your personal values, you will know what is important to you and this will help determine what you want your outcome to be. Knowing your outcome and your purpose will motivate you to take action and turn your dreams into reality.

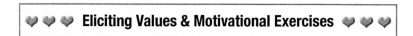

EXERCISE ONE

Eliciting Values

💜 What is important to you?

_____

_____

💜 What do you want out of life? What are you determined to do in your life?

_____

_____

_____

💜 What are you determined about at the moment?

_____

_____

💜 When are you most motivated?

_____

_____

💜 When are you most determined?

_____

_____

💜 When are you at your best?

_____

_____

Based on these questions, choose your top three values – the things you absolutely cannot imagine being without. These are the three values that give your life meaning and are the most important things in your world. For you to be truly motivated to do something, you need to make sure that you are living out your values at all times. When your values are not being met, you will not be driven.

My Top Three Values are:

_____

_____

_____

_____

_____

_____

EXERCISE TWO

Motivational Questions

❤ Name a successful person who motivates you?

_____

❤ How did they get to where they are now?

_____

_____

❤ To be motivated and successful, what do you need to do?

_____

_____

_____

❤ What needs to happen for you to be that motivated person?

_____

_____

_____

💜 How do you show that you are motivated?

_____

_____

_____

EXERCISE THREE

Motivation Anchor

💜 To get yourself into a motivated state, think about a time when you were motivated.

💜 Breathe how you breathed when you were motivated, smile the way you smiled, move the way that you moved, say the things or make the sounds you made when you were really motivated and determined to succeed.

💜 While in this state, do something unique over and over again so that you create an anchor. This anchor could be clicking your fingers and saying "I am motivated". If you keep repeating it and adding more emotional intensity to it, this will make your anchor far more powerful for yourself.

💜 Then test the anchor. Relax. Change your focus to something else and then after a minute use the anchor, clicking your fingers and saying "I am motivated" and you should feel your body going right back into that peak state of pure motivation.

EXERCISE FOUR

Be, Do, Have, Wish List

Do you remember the story of Aladdin? Aladdin rubs his magic lamp and the genie tells him that he can have three wishes. Imagine that you don't have a limit to your wishes and write down now, as many wishes as your heart desires. This is your wish list.

💜 Under **BE** write down the sort of person that you want to be.

💜 Under **DO** write the sort of things that you want to experience in your life.

💜 Under **HAVE** write down what you want to have in life.

If possible, add to this list every day and take small actions weekly to achieve your wish list.

BE	DO	HAVE
_____	_____	_____
_____	_____	_____
_____	_____	_____
_____	_____	_____
_____	_____	_____
_____	_____	_____
_____	_____	_____
_____	_____	_____
_____	_____	_____
_____	_____	_____
_____	_____	_____
_____	_____	_____
_____	_____	_____
_____	_____	_____
_____	_____	_____

Cut pictures out of the car that you want, or the TV, stereo, shoes, handbags, whatever you are aiming for, and put them up somewhere so that you can see them every day, on the fridge door, or on the wall next to the computer. When you look, say "That's my car" or "That's my TV". Visualizing these items will help to keep you motivated.

EXERCISE FIVE

Rocking Chair Test

Sit down comfortably and imagine that you are now an 80 year old woman, sitting in your rocking chair and looking back over your life. As an old lady, I want you to think about all the wonderful things that you have done throughout your life. The holidays, wild parties, the cosy nights in and the wonderful experiences that you have had with your friends and family. I want you to look back over your life and look at all the jobs that you have done and how they helped you to grow as a person.

I want you to see all the people that you have helped in your life and to see them smiling back at you. Remember all the charitable things that you have done over the years, how you have helped others who have been less fortunate and the impact that you have had on their lives.

Hear some of the profound things that people have said to you over your life and remember how those comments made you feel wonderful and alive. Take in the wonderful feelings of joy and love as you recall your life. Look at the wonderful goals that you have accomplished. Now, as you are sitting there looking back over your life, I want you to ask yourself "What do I regret not doing? What was I really passionate about but was scared to do?" I want you to now really think about this one thing that you felt you should have gone for, something that you were really passionate about. Because you did not go for that thing how disappointed do you feel?

Realise you can still do that one thing that you would have regretted not doing.

Write down now that one thing that you really want to do. Now, how will you keep yourself motivated in doing this?

_____

_____

_____

_____

_____

Imagine & You Can... Be Motivated

Visualisation time for 5 minutes every day

♥ See yourself in detail being incredibly motivated. See yourself like this in everyday life. Be the director of your own movie, where you are the star.

♥ Make the movie as perfect as possible. Imagine yourself being motivated and determined in something that you want to achieve. See how you walk when you are motivated and how you act with others who are around you. See the body language and hand gestures that you use when you are motivated.

♥ Hear the sorts of things that you say to yourself when you are really motivated and determined to do something. Hear what others say about you, when you are in this positive state.

♥ Feel how it feels when you are truly motivated and determined to succeed in life and in all that you do.

💜 Once you are satisfied, see yourself in the picture and imagine doing it for real. See what you would see, if you had this fantastic motivation and determination to succeed, hear what you would hear and notice how others respond to you.

When you are happy with your movie, store it away in the DVD collection in your mind, knowing that you can see it any time you want.

Motivational Coaching

This self coaching session will take about 30-45 minutes. Think about a goal that you want to achieve and get motivated.

G is for Goal

Think about a particular issue or challenge in your life, where you want to be more motivated. This may be in the area of career, relationships, finances, desires, achievements or any other area that is important to you.

💜 Take yourself forward in time to where the challenge has been achieved. What shows that you have achieved the goal?

_____

_____

_____

💜 How are you feeling at this point in the future?

_____

_____

💜 What are you saying to yourself?

_____

_____

💜 When do you want to be in this position that you can see in the future? Is it next week? Next month? Next year? It must be realistic.

_____

_____

_____

❤ How challenging or exciting is achieving this goal? If it is too challenging, then break it down into an element that you can achieve within the time scale that you set. If it isn't challenging enough, then you will either achieve it without trying or you will lose motivation. Do you need to add anything to make it more challenging?

_____

_____

❤ How will you know that you have achieved your goal? Is there a measurement you can use?

_____

_____

❤ Where do you have control or influence with regard to this goal?

_____

_____

R is for Reality

❤ What is happening that tells you that you have an issue and are not motivated?

_____

_____

❤ As well as what is happening, what is missing from your current situation that you would like to have?

_____

_____

❤ What have you done so far to improve things?

_____

_____

❤ What was the result you got from doing these things?

_____

_____

💜 What were the obstacles you got from doing these things?

_____

_____

💜 What other resources will you need?

_____

_____

_____

O is for Options

💜 What could you do to move yourself one step forward?

_____

_____

💜 What else could you do if you didn't have to explain what you were doing or be answerable to anybody?

_____

_____

💜 If you could devote all your time on this one thing, what would you do then?

_____

_____

_____

💜 If you went to your guardian angel for help what might she suggest?

_____

_____

💜 If money was unlimited what could you do?

_____

_____

_____

❤ What would you do if you did not have to live with the consequences?

_____

_____

❤ Choose one of the options that you think would be right for you to do now. Circle it. If you do the one thing that you have chosen, will it move you forward? If not choose something else. What is the benefit of doing this one thing?

_____

_____

_____

W is for Will

❤ What are you going to do?

_____

_____

❤ How will these actions meet your main goal?

_____

_____

_____

❤ When are you going to take these actions?

_____

_____

❤ How long do you think it will take you?

_____

_____

❤ Should anybody else be involved in this list of actions?

_____

_____

❤ What do you want this person, or these people to do?

_____

_____

❤ When will you tell them? _____

❤ Who else should know that you are doing these things?

_____

_____

❤ When will you tell them? _____

❤ Whatever your first step is, can you think of any obstacle that might stop you from doing it?

_____

_____

❤ How likely is it to stop you? If likely, what can you do to make your first step more achievable?

_____

_____

❤ How will you overcome this obstacle?

_____

_____

❤ How will you stop it from stopping you?

_____

_____

❤ Is there anything else you need to consider before you begin?

_____

_____

💜 Write down in your diary when you will have achieved your goals and when you will actually start in terms of date.

💜 On a scale of 1-10 where 10 is "I am totally committed to taking action," where are you?_____

💜 If you are not a 10 what do you need to do to make it a 10?

_____

_____

_____

Chapter Five

Be Grateful for Your Wonderful Life

*To be grateful or not to be grateful,
that is the question.*

*Gratitude: to feel thankful and to
appreciate kindness.*

In this Chapter you will:

💜 Learn how to be grateful for your life

💜 Learn how to consistently experience positive feelings

💜 Create the life that you want with the power of visualisation

💜 Transform your life with your own magical powers

Transform Your Life with Gratitude

This chapter will transform your life. Master this emotion and you can guarantee that your future will be filled with love, joy and inner peace, even at times of sadness. Sincere gratitude empowers you to focus on the positive aspects of your life. It lets you develop greater awareness and appreciation of overlooked but important little things that make up life. Gratitude is a powerful process for transforming your energy and bringing more of what you want into your life. Be grateful for what you already have and you will attract more good things into your life.

When you are consistently experiencing positive feelings, your subconscious mind will start to form a more creative flow state. This lets you imagine and create the life you want. It is impossible to bring more into your life if you are feeling ungrateful for what you have. This is because the thoughts and feelings that you emit, if you feel ungrateful, are negative emotions. Whether it is resentment, jealousy or dissatisfaction, those feelings won't bring you what you want. However, a positive state of mind will broaden your horizons of creativity and will bring into your life more of what you deserve.

Being grateful will help strengthen any relationships you have. When you appreciate somebody, it makes them feel good about themselves and you will both naturally feel more compassion and warmth for each other. You can't have love without gratitude.

So What can You be Grateful for?

There are a million and one things to be grateful for. So many of us don't stop to think about all the wonderful people in our lives, the beautiful places that surround us and the magical times that take place. But we are so lucky in having this fantastic world to live in. There are so many different places to explore and thousands of incredible places to see. Just imagine some of the experiences you could encounter now. You could go swimming with the dolphins in the dazzling blue seas of the Caribbean, go on exciting safari adventures and encounter the wild beasts in their natural habitat, chill out and have a relaxing time in the sand dunes in the French Riviera, go shopping in the hustle and bustle of the vibrant city of New York, go skiing on the crisp white snow in Canada, go clubbing and dance your socks off until the early hours in the morning with friends in Ibiza and then watch the sun rise whilst lying on the soft sands of the beach. There is an abundance of events waiting to take place in your life, so be grateful.

Be grateful for all the experiences that you have had. Listening to captivating stories from your parents' past, sharing that first lingering and sensual kiss that made you feel like you were going to explode inside, laughing so hard with your friends that your sides felt like they were going to split, walking along the beach with the wet sand underneath your feet and etching your name into the sand with a big stick. There are so many phenomenal memories that you can be grateful for.

Also, be grateful for the smaller things in life – smelling the fresh fragrance of flowers, watching the sun set, listening to the birds singing first thing in the morning, catching up with your friends, hugging a loved one, having a meaningful conversation with somebody… all of these are moments you can be grateful for.

Being grateful makes you feel alive inside, it makes you happy and fulfilled. It will make an enormous difference to your life.

When is it Hard to be Grateful?

There will always be circumstances cropping up that you might think of as hard to cope with. The major challenge in life is to be able to deal with these tricky experiences. You will continuously learn lessons from all the tough times in your life and consequently you will become a better person. Be thankful for your life, even when times are hard. I know that it might seem impossible to be grateful when you are ill or someone has dumped you or maybe even died, but there is always a silver lining to every cloud.

Illness

A few years ago, I became friends with a wonderful young woman called Helwyn, who has been a huge source of inspiration to me, in writing this chapter. We met in the gym, when Helwyn was using the treadmill next to me. I had never seen her in the gym before and I said hello. The next thing I knew, we were engrossed in conversation. I liked her instantly. She was warm, fun and full of energy. Then our conversation finally came around to what we did as work. I told Helwyn what I did and then waited for her to tell me what she did.

In a matter of a fact way, she said she didn't work any more as she had cancer. I was dumbstruck. I couldn't believe that someone so positive, happy and full of energy could be seriously ill. It didn't make sense to me.

Helwyn told me that she had been diagnosed with breast cancer two years ago. After having chemotherapy sessions and a mastectomy, sadly the doctors found that the cancer had spread to her liver and her bones. Helwyn is regularly having chemotherapy sessions and we are, of course, all hoping that they work and she becomes well again.

The strange thing is, to look at her, you'd think she didn't have a care in the world and was perfectly healthy. Funny how deceptive appearances are!

What Helwyn said to me about her illness has stuck with me, and I want to pass it on here:

"I've learnt a lot from being ill and here's the biggest lesson. How long your life is isn't important – but what you do with it is. Live life to the full and enjoy every minute of it.

Appreciate the small things. Be grateful for your friends and your wonderful family. Be grateful that you are healthy enough to do all the things that you do. Have fun. Be grateful for all the beautiful animals and birds that you see outside. Be amazed by the beauty of this world. Be excited that you can feel the warmth of the sun on your back and can hear the sound of the rain beating down on the rooftops. Take note and appreciate everything now. Make every moment in life count, as you will never get that moment back."

What an amazing person! She is so unselfish. She also said that by having this illness, she has been able to support other terminally ill people and this has given her a sense of purpose. She has found good in something that is so horrible. She is grateful that she can help others. She is grateful that she, and not her family, has got this disease. Unbelievable!

I have learnt a lot from Helwyn. I have learnt that even when you are seriously ill, you can still be grateful and happy. By focusing on happy and magical moments, you are able to change the way that you feel and hence the quality of your life. I will always be thankful for meeting Helwyn.

If ever you are feeling run down and need to take time off school, university or work, then make the most of your sick days. Do what Helwyn does and think about things that you can be grateful for. Reflect on what is going on in your life. Most of the time, people do not give themselves the time to assess their lives; to think about what they want out of their lives, whether they are happy, what would make them happier, what is going right in their lives. When you are at home in bed or lying on the sofa trying to get better, use your time wisely to be grateful and think about your life.

Many of my clients and friends have done some of their most profound thinking when they are ill. It gives you the opportunity to sit down and think about your situation. Even think about what actually made you ill. Assess whether you need to slow down, change your diet or give up some of those negative behaviours to be healthier and live the life that you deserve. Next time you are poorly, don't feel wretched about life and think woe is me, ask yourself "What has made me ill?" What do I need to do to be healthy? Your body will know and your inner voice will tell you what to do. Use your time to think positive thoughts.

Negative Attitudes

It's hard to feel gratitude when you've practised negative thoughts for so long. But it's equally difficult to feel it when you're surrounded by negative people. Negative people weigh us down. They can make us feel low and all our good feelings of gratitude are swept away. If you are somebody who is ungrateful then it's time you asked yourself better questions, to allow you to be more appreciative. Ask yourself, What can I be grateful for?

What should I be grateful for? Who should I be grateful to? These sorts of questions will always bring out the positive side in us.

Decide whether you really want pessimistic people in your life. If you do, then offer them some advice. Tell them to lighten up and feed their minds with positive uplifting books, music, films, anything that will make their spirits come alive. If you don't, then spring clean the negative people out of your life.

Relationship Split ups

Splitting up with a loved one can be incredibly painful. When we split up with somebody, we either feel grateful that we are out of the relationship or we feel hurt and often rejected.

Having a successful relationship is about having true love for yourself and being able to love another, being able to respect that person and having heartfelt understanding for them. This takes time and a lot of effort and being in a relationship is a commitment, one that you shouldn't take lightly. If you have split up with a partner, think about the things that you have learnt from the relationship. Think realistically, not idealistically, about your time together and what was good and bad. Think about what you want to be different from a man, next time. There will be things you want to be different; otherwise you would still be with him. Nature has a funny way of letting us know whether something is right or wrong. So learn from your past relationships. Be grateful that you have been taught from experience, so that next time you will find somebody who is better for you. It might take you a few attempts to get the man of your dreams, but if you are really focused on getting the perfect relationship, then you will. *Imagine & You Can...*

Death

Have you ever lost someone very close to you? Have you ever felt that you've been cheated and that it wasn't fair and that life was cruel? A few years ago, a friend of mine, died from leukaemia at the age of 27. I was incredibly upset. My immediate thoughts were that it was so unfair. How could this happen to such a wonderful person, when she had so much of her life ahead of her? I felt cheated and started to totally question my faith in life. I found it very difficult to cope with, at first, until my stepfather, Charles, sat down with me and helped me to change my feelings about the situation.

Charles asked me two very significant questions that made me really rethink things through. First, he asked me whether my friend would want me to be sad forever and not to live my life to the full. I thought about it and immediately thought no. Then he asked me if I could have an alternative meaning that would make her death more positive to me? A tricky question - how could there ever be a positive meaning from somebody dying?

However, I did think some more and I came up with a more positive meaning. My friend was an incredibly kind, honest, loving person and her greatest gift was that she was so unselfish. She loved helping her friends feel good about themselves and was always so cheerful. It suddenly dawned on me that instead of feeling bitter because she was not around anymore, why not imagine that she is with me all the time, as my guardian angel. I know it might sound a bit silly but this has been very comforting for me. I often imagine that she is flying next to me and is helping me to be a better person. Certainly for me, having my own guardian angel helped me to get over my friend's death.

Many events happen in people's lives that we term as bad, such as illness, death, failing exams, not getting the jobs that we want and relationship split ups. Often, it is very difficult for people to feel grateful and happy throughout these times. The only way that we can feel happy during such circumstances is to stop focusing on what is making us sad and low. Seek alternative meanings.

When you are grateful you are at peace with the world. I have learnt that it is too easy to allow your mind to slip into negativity. When this happens we lose our sense of gratitude. We then take people in our lives for granted and the love that we feel is replaced with resentment and frustration. Being grateful gets rid of all the negative emotions.

There are so many things you could be grateful for – and should be. I have met so many people in my life who appear to have everything but are not grateful, and so they are unfulfilled and miserable. When you are grateful you are happy and stress-free.

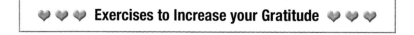

❤ ❤ ❤ **Exercises to Increase your Gratitude** ❤ ❤ ❤

EXERCISE ONE

Grateful for my Loved Ones

Write down all the people to whom you are grateful in your life and why you love them so much.

_____

_____

_____

_____

_____

_____

_____

EXERCISE TWO

Grateful for my Health

Write down what it is that you are grateful for, about your health. Even if you are not 100% healthy, start saying "thank you" for what you have got and this will help you to get what you desire most.

_____

_____

_____

_____

_____

_____

_____

EXERCISE THREE

Wake Up & Be Grateful For Two Minutes

Every morning, for two minutes, before you get out of bed, you are going to say aloud what you are grateful for in your life. Start the day, thinking of all the things that are fantastic in your life and that you want to thank the world for. By being grateful, you will start to have that warm feeling inside. By being grateful you will feel fulfilled.

EXERCISE FOUR

Keep a Thank You Journal

Keep a Thank You journal. Every day, write down a few things that you are thankful for. This will bring you to being truly grateful. After a few days of practising being thankful, you will find it easier and more natural to appreciate the beauty in your life

EXERCISE FIVE

Create the Life that you Want with Visualisation

By being grateful, you will now start to attract more of the "good things" into your life. When you give out positive feelings your subconscious mind will enter more easily into a flow state, where-by you can start creating fantastically vivid dreams and plans. By imagining what you want, you will automatically find ways of creating it. And if you master visualising and imagining what you want, you can create anything.

Visualisation is applied imagination. You make a mental creation of what you want and then make it physically happen. The technique of visualisation has been used for hundreds of years, as an incredibly powerful way of training the human mind. It really is a fantastic way of changing your life. Visualising literally means "seeing" in your mind's eye what you want. Imagine the sort of life you want and how you want to feel. So many people say that they cannot visualise, but everyone can. Can you remember what you wore yesterday? What colours were you wearing? Were you wearing any patterns? By remembering what you actually wore, you had to visualise these clothes. We do visualise, we just don't realise we're doing it.

When you believe in yourself anything is possible. Imagine being in control of your life, being happy, successful, talented and lucky *and this is what you will be*. Choose to see yourself as this, behave as if you are this and you will become this. Whatever you focus on consistently is what you get and what you become. Start being creative about what you want in your life. Have a grand vision. Be excited. Be playful. Wonder what would happen if... Dare to let yourself imagine so you can...

When you believe in yourself anything is possible

If film producers, artists, authors, painters, actors and songwriters didn't use their imagination, we wouldn't have all the fantastic films, songs, books, paintings and TV programmes that we have to immerse our lives into and use as escapism in every day life.

I remember reading that Victoria Beckham had set out to be more famous than Ariel washing powder. Is she? I think so! Victoria Beckham is a classic example of a star who set out with a vision and a dream. By making her vision so compelling, she took action and produced the fame she wanted.

Mohammad Ali – the world's greatest boxer – always used the power of visualisation to get what he wanted. Days before he stepped into the ring, he would picture himself at the end of the fight, with his arm held aloft by the referee, proclaiming him the champion. He would visualise this with utter commitment and belief. He would hear the crowds cheering, feel the heat in his body and know that he was the winner. All his energy would then be directed into making this happen. He would never think about the start, just the overall outcome of his winning. From that time until the end of the fight his subconscious mind would be constantly looking out for things that would make this outcome true.

I use visualisation all the time. Before I go into any situation, I imagine how I want the event to happen. 99% of the time, it goes how I want it to. For instance, if I am going to a meeting, then I imagine a fantastic outcome. I imagine the person I'm meeting to be nodding and smiling and enjoying herself. I imagine us having great rapport and that we come to an agreement where we both benefit.

Recently, I had a voicemail message from a prospective client saying that she was interested in coaching, as she wanted to increase her confidence. Before I rang her back, I visualised how the telephone call would go. I imagined us having a conversation about where her insecurities lay, where she would like more confidence, how she would like to feel and be. I imagined us talking about how I could help her move forward to improve her confidence and then her saying she would like to go ahead. This is exactly what happened. Without a shadow of a doubt, visualisation does work!

If at any time you doubt your ability to be creative, remember that five or six times a night, you create an entirely new dream, which you not only script, but act in, direct and watch. This creation is so effortless that most people don't realise it but remember that you can create anything in your life that you want.

❤ ❤ ❤ VISUALISATION EXERCISES ❤ ❤ ❤

Start Visualising What You Want, To Create The Life That You Desire

The next set of exercises are daydreaming exercises. For each exercise, you need to allow yourself five minutes, where you can sit down and start imagining how you want your life to be, in all areas. Do these every day and you will be able to take control, and create the life you want.

❤ Imagine Your Day, Every Day

We all have "to do" lists, and thoughts and ideas of what we will do day-to-day. But now, I want you to set up your day before you get out of bed, so that it is perfect.

Imagine having a fabulous day. Visualise yourself being happy and having fun at the start of every day. What sort of things will be happening today? What sort of people will you be with? How will you make them happy? What sort of activities will you be doing? Who will you smile at? What success will you have at school or in your job? How will you respond to people? Imagine people smiling at you and being grateful that you've helped them. Imagine that your day is a perfect day.

💜 Imagine How Your Next Year Will Be

Your brain does not know the difference between whether you have done something or not. Everything that has happened in your life was created internally as a thought, feeling, movie or picture. Use your mind to create what you want to happen this year. Where do you want to be? What sort of job do you want? Do you want to go travelling? Where will you be living? What will you be learning about and studying? Will you meet any famous people? Who will you spend most of your time with? Will you be helping others to feel good and happy about themselves?

💜 Imagine Your Life Over The Next Five Years

Where will you be? Will you have your own business? What sort of salary will you be earning? Where will you live? Will you have a big garden and a swimming pool? Will you have pets? Will you have a boyfriend or be married? Will you have children? Will you have a fancy car? What will your relationships be like with your friends and family? Imagine the life that you want and you can have it – just get it clear exactly what you want.

💜 Imagine How You Want To Look

Visualise what you want your body to look like. Imagine you are strong and healthy. How do you want to look? What do you want to feel like? Picture yourself in perfect health. Imagine yourself looking fantastic naked and being comfortable in your own skin. Imagine yourself going into your wardrobe and picking out your clothes effortlessly, as everything looks great on you. Imagine yourself being totally comfortable around food and happy with who you are.

💜 Imagine Yourself In A Loving Relationship

Imagine yourself in a relationship where both of you are as equally happy and very passionate about one another. Imagine yourself being blissfully in love and spending time with your boyfriend. What sort of activities will you do together? How would you make each other happy? Imagine yourself smiling and laughing. Imagine both of you being totally honest with each other and being compassionate to one another.

❤ Imagine Yourself Being Motivated

Visualise yourself being incredibly motivated in your life and living your life with absolute passion. See yourself being excited as you get up in the morning, knowing you're going to do something worthwhile that you enjoy. See yourself being motivated in living the life that you want. What would you be motivated in doing? How would you be different to who you are now? See yourself smiling, jumping around, your eyes bright and sparkly as you share your enthusiasm and love with others. See yourself motivating and making everyone else around you happy and at ease with themselves.

❤ Imagine Being Happy

See yourself as happy and content. Happy being on your own and enjoying your own company, reading, daydreaming, walking outside at one with nature. See yourself happy with your family, loved ones, out with friends, doing activities, on holiday, shopping, running or horse riding. What would happiness look like, sound like and feel like?

❤ Imagine Yourself Confident

See yourself as confident. Somebody who can walk into a room and keep their head held high. See yourself talking to people with great eye contact, being smiley and interested in them. See yourself as being approachable and someone who looks like they're happy. See your body language being open, shoulders back, standing up straight and with bright eyes and a dazzling smile. How would this make you feel? Would this make a difference to your life?

❤ Imagine Yourself Helping Others

See yourself as helping others and getting joy out of making others happy. By making others happy, you will make yourself happy. Nothing will actually make you happier than giving to others. See their faces when you give them that little bit of time so they can share a story with you. Spend a few more minutes on the phone to your parents, so they can tell you what they have been up to, as opposed to you doing all the talking. By trying to understand others and listening to them properly, they will feel appreciated and loved. You will be contributing to society by putting others before yourself and being compassionate. See yourself helping people who are needy. See yourself as a good person – and this is what you will be.

Chapter Six

Be Happy - Always

*To be happy or not to be happy,
that is the question.*

*Happiness: a feeling showing pleasure
or contentment.*

In this Chapter you will:

♥ Find out what happiness means to you

♥ Focus on happy thoughts

♥ Find out what makes you happy

♥ Create an action plan to make you happy NOW

Happiness

"Happiness!" Just saying the word aloud lights up my soul. How does it make you feel? Say it aloud now – "happiness". What thoughts do you have? What sensations do you get in your body? Does it make you feel happy and alive?

The word "happiness" makes me smile. Like most people, I have connected fantastic thoughts to this word.

What does happiness mean to you? Would you say you're a happy person? Do you laugh and have fun? If not, you can change this now.

Most people think that they'll only experience happiness when a particular condition or state is reached – when they're a size 10, or have passed their exams, or are more confident at work, or have the man of their dreams, or win the lottery. But the reality is simple – your happiness does not depend on getting or having what you want.

Happiness is the process of creating and experiencing good feelings in your body and mind, moment by moment. When you recognise that happiness is a process, you can ultimately master it. *You* decide whether or not *you* are going to experience happiness.

To feel happy now, all you need to do is to focus on good thoughts and think about things that make you smile. From the information and memories that are available to you, select only the good parts to make you feel joyous. The better you feel, the better the stories you tell yourself and the more positive your perspective will be. The better the stories you tell yourself about your life, the easier it is to take better actions and the better you will feel. Whatever you do consistently, you get better at. If you consistently shut down emotions, you will get better at feeling depressed. But if you practise focusing on giving yourself better feelings and telling yourself happy stories you will get better and better at feeling happy. The secret to happiness is having blissful thoughts and memories.

Happy Hour

I recently worked with a girl called Amanda who was suffering from depression. As soon as she walked into my office, I could tell from her posture that she was depressed – she was walking slowly, her shoulders were drooped and she wasn't making eye contact.

Amanda had come to me for some NLP transformation and coaching work, so that she could learn how to be happy again. Amanda had been depressed for nearly five months and had forgotten how to be happy. When you do or feel something every day, such as learning to drive or feeling happy, it will gradually become second nature without your having to think about it. This is what I felt was happening with Amanda and her depression.

Imagine one day you wake up feeling a bit down. It's dark and raining outside, you don't want to go to work and you feel depressed and miserable. You plough through the day and are glad when it's over.

The next morning, when you wake up, you feel slightly better. But when something goes wrong later on that morning, you start to think immediately about how miserable you felt the day before, and start dwelling on that too. You feel down and wonder what can go wrong next. You are starting to think more miserable thoughts than happy thoughts. Your brain hallucinates about horrible things that could go wrong and the rest of the day you feel depressed.

The next day you wake up in a dark mood, due to all the negative thoughts from yesterday. You automatically begin to tell yourself miserable stories and focus on unpleasant experiences. You keep asking yourself, "why me?" and little by little you feel worse and worse. This keeps on happening repeatedly, like a vicious circle and slowly but surely you become proficient at making yourself feel unhappy.

If you practise having happy thoughts, you will turn into a happier person

It is vital that you are aware of your habitual thoughts. If you find yourself thinking negatively, you need to change this immediately. You don't want to become great at being depressed! Likewise, if you practise having happy thoughts and being grateful, you will turn into a happier person. In your mind, only select and replay the joyful memories to make yourself feel good.

In our session, I asked Amanda to explain to me how she would know when she was happy. She replied, "I will know because I'll be smiling again. I'll feel energetic and I'll feel light, instead of being weighed down." It is important that Amanda knew what being happy meant to her. *We all have different ideas of what happiness means to us and it is crucial that we have clarity of what we truly want to feel like, so we can attain this.*

I wanted to help Amanda experience happiness again, and the first thing to do was to help her to remember how to feel this. In our session, she needed to imagine and pretend that she was happy, even if she didn't feel it. This would allow her nervous system to remember what it felt like and looked like to be happy.

This was terrific, but she was only halfway there. To be happy you need to not only have a strong and upright body posture, you also need an excellent psychology. That was next on the agenda.

Amanda's mindset was currently very negative and of course this was not helping her. She had failed her A-levels the year before and didn't get into university with all her friends. She felt like a failure repeating sixth form, and she was lonely because all her friends were now away at university. To try and make herself feel better, she started to comfort eat and was now putting on lots of weight, which made her feel even more miserable. In fact, the only positive aspect she could see in her life was her great relationship with her boyfriend. By Amanda not going away to university, their relationship had developed and was now very strong.

"I first felt incredibly down when my friends went off to their respective universities," said Amanda. *"I couldn't stop crying as I felt so lonely. Every day, I would cry and eventually my parents took me to the doctor as they were concerned about my wellbeing. The doctor instantly told me that I was suffering from depression and prescribed me some antidepressants. The doctor assured me that these would cure me. Having seen the doctor, I actually felt worse, as I now felt that I had real issues and was a depressant."*

Having been told by the doctor that she was depressed, Amanda started to feel even more so. The way people see us and label us often gives us a new identity. Our self identity affects how we behave. If we identify ourselves as somebody who is depressed, then we will behave like this. If we see ourselves as somebody who is positive and happy, we will behave that way. In Amanda's case, she had taken on the identity of a depressed person, and this was keeping her feeling depressed.

During my session with Amanda, she became aware of what she was doing (playing out the role she had been given by the doctor) and knew that it was time to stop this behaviour. By being aware, Amanda stopped identifying herself as a depressed person.

Amanda now had to start feeling better about her life, and the only way to do this was to have a new outlook on it. (However, if you are very depressed, to the extent where even this is very difficult or impossible, please see your GP urgently. He or she can recommend some sort of therapy or remedy, to help you feel better in the meantime.)

Amanda came up with the following more positive points of view for her life:

- By living at home and waiting a year to go to university, she was able to save money for this event.

- Instead of concentrating on missing her friends, she planned to visit her friends and have mini breaks. Staying with her friends and experiencing different places was suddenly very exciting for her.

- By staying at school for another year, she could make even more friends.

- By retaking the year, she could achieve really good grades, as she knew what to expect and was more determined this time around.

- By staying at home she could spend more time with her family, whom she really loved and got on well with.

💜 Having put on weight, she now had a valid reason for her boyfriend to go salsa dancing with her. Although her boyfriend did not really want to salsa dance, he had said that he would do this with Amanda, to help her to lose weight. This was great, as she could learn how to dance as well as spending quality time with her boyfriend.

By looking at her life in a different way, Amanda felt much better. You could see the transformation as she spoke throughout our session. Amanda became livelier, started using positive physiology and smiled lots. By the end of our session, she looked like a different person. She realized she had complete control over her life and how she felt. She felt that the big weight had been lifted off her shoulders as she was choosing to be happy now.

Shifting your focus can change the way you think and feel in a moment. You need to be aware of what's going on in your mind. You need to be aware of what makes you sad and what makes you happy. Then, most importantly, focus on the happy thoughts.

Notice the Good

All people view the world differently and we all have different ways of processing our experiences. Two people can be at the same lunch event and can have a totally different experience to one another because of what they have focused on. If you're in a bad mood, you might start looking for all the things that you don't like about the restaurant, the meal and even the people you are with.

But if you're in a good mood, you will automatically look for the good in others and the things around you, as you are processing good thoughts. The trick is to start noticing the small things in life from *now on*, to make you feel good. Notice the sun shining down on you, hear the birds singing, see the wonderful expressions on other people's faces, listen and appreciate the nice words others say to you, feel the wind blowing in your face. Recognise all these small things and give thanks for them. Appreciate the small things in life and you will instantly feel happy and have a more positive perspective on life. Always remember "Beauty is in the eye of the beholder."

Outside Influences

Increasing your happiness with joyful thoughts will always work for you. Be aware that there are, of course, some other very important factors that contribute to your happiness, such as diet/nutrition, exercise, rest, environment and outside interests. All these factors have a direct effect on your biochemistry. They can help increase endorphins and other good chemicals in the brain's cranial fluid, which strengthens your happiness.

Diet & Nutrition

Everything that you eat and drink is a chemical, which affects your performance and how you feel. Think about how you feel the next day if you have drunk too much alcohol. Or observe how a person's behaviour changes when they have drunk too much. Think about how children will suddenly turn hyperactive having had excessive E numbers and sugars or caffeine. All these chemicals impact on us. When we eat and drink things that are highly concentrated in sugars and fats, we feel sluggish and low. However, when we eat foods that are natural and have the right chemicals in them, we will feel vibrant, full of energy and happy. Eat wisely and in moderation.

Exercise

Your body has been designed for you to move. We function at our best when we do physical exertion, so that we can remove any toxins and more importantly secrete the beneficial endorphins that we need to make us feel good. Next time you feel a little low, take some exercise and see how much better you feel afterwards. Even a brisk walk for twenty minutes or half an hour will be enough for this to work. If you can do some form of exercise every day, you will not only increase your self-esteem, look good, be physically and mentally fit, but you will feel far happier in yourself. Exercise increases your physical and mental fitness.

Rest

Sufficient rest is essential for your body to eliminate toxins and rejuvenate itself. Have you ever noticed that you sleep more when you are depressed than when you are happy? Sleep will help you keep your mind and body balanced, helping to keep you emotionally stable.

Environment

Surround yourself with people who are exuberant and vibrant, as this will help you to stay happier. People can zap your energy easily and it is important to protect your positive energy. I surround myself with positive people and I believe that I am very blessed, as I have superb friends, family and clients in my life. I do sometimes come across clients who are negative, but because my energy is more dominant and stronger than theirs, I am rarely affected by negative vibes.

Have you been affected by negativity? Have you got any friends who constantly moan, groan and grumble about absolutely everything? Do they get you down? When negative or even sad people get together they can really cause you to feel low. One of the most sorrowful experiences that I have had was at the time of Princess Diana's death in 1997. I was absolutely astonished by the way the nation, and indeed many overseas countries too, were affected. I always admired Diana as she was such a giving soul, but I didn't know her on a personal level and was not a devoted fan. Nevertheless, I was shocked by her death. It took me a while to realize that I was sensing the feelings of the nation. So many people had been affected deeply by sadness and the energy of sorrow was being swept across the country.

People's energies affect us and there is no denying this. Sometimes, we cannot escape negative energy, as in the case of Princess Diana's death, but if we can try to surround ourselves with positive people and upbeat environments, this can help.

Outside Pursuits

Choose to be happy and choose meaningful hobbies to make you feel great.

It's hugely important that you spend your time doing pleasurable things, to make you feel better, to take time out for yourself and do things that will make you happy. For instance, having a relaxing bath, sitting in bed all warm and cosy reading a good book, writing your own journal, thinking about what you can do to make yourself and others feel happier, exercising to increase your energy, having a facial, massage and generally pampering yourself. Whatever makes you feel good, do it.

Think about what interests you have that make you feel alive and happy? Have you thought about trying out a new hobby? It is often great fun having a go at different experiences. I have had some of my most magical moments trying out new sports, learning to salsa dance and also going to different holiday destinations.

You now have the right ingredients to be happy. You can choose whether you want to be happy or not. If you focus on all the good things that are happening, you will ultimately feel pleasure. Replay good memories and you will experience joy, time and time again. Living a balanced lifestyle and surrounding yourself with positive people and meaningful hobbies will aid your happiness.

❤ ❤ ❤ **Happiness Exercises** ❤ ❤ ❤

EXERCISE ONE

What Made You Happy Today?

At the end of the day, spend a few minutes making a list of all the good things that happened and what made you happy. Even if it was a smile from a stranger, recover the experience and relive it. In this way, you will build up the habit of noticing what is good in your life.

What Made You Happy Today?

_____

_____

_____

_____

_____

_____

_____

_____

_____

EXERCISE TWO

Remember Good Memories

Write down ten really good memories that you have that make you feel wonderful inside. These can be anything from your first kiss, walking in the sunshine, dancing in a club, sightseeing with your friends and so on.

_____

_____

_____

_____

_____

_____

_____

_____

_____

_____

EXERCISE THREE

Who Else Is Happy?

Write down a list of positive and happy people with whom you love spending time and why it makes you happy being with them. Ring or email each person over the course of the next week and arrange a time that you can get together with them in the near future, so that you spend your time with people that fill you with joy.

_____

_____

_____

_____

_____

_____

_____

EXERCISE FOUR

What Makes You Happy?

Write down a list of all the things that you like doing in your spare time and that give your life meaning. Commit to doing at least two of your pleasurable hobbies each week.

_____

_____

_____

_____

_____

_____

_____

EXERCISE FIVE

Changes to be Made

Act on things that annoy or bother you. Don't keep going over events in your mind or tell others about them. Every time you repeat something, you ingrain it into your subconscious mind. When a person, a role or a situation continues to make you unhappy, angry or uncomfortable, find a way to change it. You don't have to ignore it or put your head in the sand – just find a way to deal with it and then don't dwell on it.

Write down any person, role or situation that is making you unhappy and decide how you are going to change this today.

_____

_____

_____

_____

_____

_____

EXERCISE SIX

Imagine & You Can... Be Happy

Visualisation time for 5 minutes every day

- See yourself in detail, being incredibly happy and content. See yourself like this in everyday life. Be the director of your own movie, where you are the star.

- Make the movie as perfect as possible. Imagine yourself being happy and content in all situations of your life. See how you walk when you are happy and how you act with others who are around you. See the body language and hand gestures that you use when you are in good spirits.

- Hear the sort of things that you say to yourself when you are on cloud nine. Hear what others say about you, when you are in this positive state.

- Feel how it feels when you are truly euphoric.

- Once you are satisfied, see yourself in your movie and imagine doing it for real. See what you will see when you are joyous, hear what you will hear and notice how others respond to you.

When you are happy with your movie, store it away in the DVD collection in your mind, knowing that you can see it any time that you want.

Happy Questions

💜 How do you know when you're happy?

_____

_____

_____

💜 What does it feel like for you?

_____

_____

_____

💜 What does being happy look like to you?

_____

_____

💜 What can you hear when you're happy? What are you saying to yourself?

_____

_____

💜 Write down as many ways as possible that would help you to create more happiness.

_____

_____

_____

_____

_____

💜 What would you need to have more happiness in your life?

_____

_____

_____

💜 How much control do you have over your happiness?

_____

_____

💜 How do you control your happiness?

_____

_____

💜 Could you commit to making your life happier now? What will you do?

_____

_____

_____

💜 What do you have to do to allow yourself to be happier?

_____

_____

_____

💜 On a scale of 1-10 where 10 is "excellent", where would you rate your happiness? Where are you now? What could you do to make it a 10?

_____

_____

_____

💜 How can you keep being happy, even when something unpleasant happens?

_____

_____

_____

💜 What can you do to not let something affect you?

_____

_____

_____

♥ What contingency plans do you need in place so that you can still stay happy and not be sad/miserable?

_____

_____

_____

_____

Create a Happy Hour Action Plan

♥ What could you do now to get in the right frame of mind?

_____

_____

_____

_____

♥ What can you do with your body to help you feel happier?

_____

_____

_____

♥ What sort of language/imagery could you use that is more positive?

_____

_____

_____

_____

♥ What questions can you ask yourself to put you in a great mood? – i.e. what makes me happy?

_____

_____

_____

_____

💜 How are you going to create more happiness from now on in your life?

_____

_____

_____

_____

💜 What will you do from now on at home and in college/work to ensure that you are happy? How will you know that you are happy?

_____

_____

_____

💜 How will you stick to this?

_____

_____

_____

💜 How will this help you have a better life?

_____

_____

_____

_____

Chapter Seven

Have an Outstanding Relationship

To be in love or not to be in love,
that is the question.

Love: an intense feeling of deep affection and
sexual attachment to someone.

In this Chapter you will:

💜 Find how you want your relationship to be

💜 Find out whether you are with the right person

💜 Discover ways to increase your love NOW

💜 Learn how to have a blissful relationship

Feeling Wonderful

Love is a truly wonderful feeling. When you feel love for somebody, it feels as if every fibre of your being overflows with energy and warmth. Love is sacred and deep down we all want a loving relationship. It's only natural. Having good times and love with another person takes you to the top of the barometer of good feelings.

In this chapter, you will not only learn how to create a loving relationship but how to achieve the feelings that you want. You will also become aware of what stops you having the relationships that you want and how to overcome these hurdles.

Over the years, I have had a few serious relationships but none of them were ever truly fulfilling because I was so unhappy in myself and also because I did not know how to create the perfect relationship. This area of my life, I am proud to say, is now absolutely fabulous. Having a wonderful and loving relationship is my biggest achievement to date.

Having always wanted a superb relationship, two years ago I decided to invest nearly all my time and energy in learning how to have a more loving relationship. I have read numerous books on how to have better relationships, as well as talking and learning from people whom I know who have great relationships and finding out their secrets. The advice that I offer you in this chapter will help you to create a loving relationship in your own life.

Love

I personally don't think there is a better feeling than love. When you fall in love, you feel as if you are on the top of the world. All your friends and family want to know what happy pills you have been taking, as you are so ecstatic.

There is no greater feeling than love! Yet, if this is something we all want, then why have we not all got it? Let's explore what is stopping you from having a loving relationship, so that you can make the necessary changes to get that perfect love.

If you are not in a Relationship or don't have the Relationship that you deserve then it may be because:

💜 *You don't love yourself enough and so can never give to the relationship totally*

💜 *You have not clearly stated or thought about what you want your relationship to be like*

💜 *You have very negative beliefs about relationships and need to work on these to believe that you can have the relationship you want*

💜 *You have not got the right partner and need to readdress your relationship*

💜 *You need to learn to put your partner first*

Self-Love First

Love and accept yourself first, and then you can fully give yourself to a relationship

It is impossible to have a fulfilling and totally loving relationship until you really love yourself. You will know whether or not you love yourself and you will also know that if you don't, this is having a dramatic effect on your relationships. If you have insecurities in yourself, this will definitely manifest itself in your relationships or lack of them. If you doubt yourself and put yourself down, then you will not believe what your partner tells you.

When you love yourself properly, you will be able to see all your good traits. You know who you are and what you deserve and want from life. This in turn allows you to be able to see the same in others. If you consistently focus on the positive elements of yourself you will also concentrate on the good points in other people. This makes it a lot easier for you to like and also to love others. However, if you are always paying attention to the negative points about yourself, you will automatically find yourself pointing out the bad in others too. This makes it very hard to truly love another person properly.

So many people who don't love themselves will try to get love from another person. But, if you don't love yourself, you will never truly believe that your partner loves you.

Imagine it, your partner tells you that he loves you. Although you want to believe it, you can't because deep down you don't think that there is anything about you to love. And when he pays you a compliment you don't believe him. You find it incredibly uncomfortable to accept a compliment, as your subconscious mind is telling you differently.

Every time he tells you something nice, you don't believe him, so eventually he stops saying nice things to you and becomes despondent. Why? Because he is finding it embarrassing saying these things and you are consistently throwing them back in his face, as though he is wrong. He feels like a failure because his kind words aren't making a difference.

Now you are wondering why he doesn't pay you compliments any more and you think he's gone off you. You become clingy, as you are craving reassurance from him, which he is not giving you. You have been pushing him away due to your own self doubt. You now question him when he goes out, as you are becoming paranoid that he will meet somebody else. There is no trust between you both and the relationship cannot carry on in this unhealthy way and a few months down the line it ends.

I know this, because I have been there. This happened to me for years on end. I entered relationships, hoping my new boyfriend would make me feel good about myself. At first he did but after the initial excitement of the relationship had worn off, it *always* went down hill. Because I didn't love myself, I started to question his love and doubted whether he actually fancied me. Every relationship ended due to my lack of self-love. Until you love yourself, your relationship will never be how you want it, as you will always doubt your partner.

These sorts of scenarios happen to countless people all over the world. Don't fall into the same trap. A truly healthy relationship will give both people a heightened appreciation of magic and love. When you enter a relationship with an immense amount of emotional emptiness, you risk creating pain for yourself and your partner. It is vital that you love yourself in order to have a loving and blissful relationship. You will be able to accept love and warmth from your partner and in return you will be able to reciprocate his love.

Declare How You Want Your Relationship To Be
Clearly state and think about what you want your relationship to be like.

Why is it that we spend countless hours researching what TV or holiday we are going to buy but don't put the same time into finding the right person for ourselves? You must invest the same sort of consideration and care into planning and deciding how you want your relationship to be, which is far more important. Instead of plunging into a relationship and finding yourself quickly disappointed, shop around and give yourself time to know what you want in a man.

Most of us don't think about the relationship that we want; in fact we spend more time thinking about what we don't want. Of course you have heard your friends or family moan that they go for the wrong type of man? Typically you hear the phrase, "what is wrong with me that I keep attracting the wrong sort of man?"

If you keep thinking about what you don't want, you will end up with the same result again and again because your subconscious mind has no idea what you are searching for. Shift your focus and think about the sort of man and relationship that would fulfil you, then you will get just this.

By knowing what you want, you are able to find or create this. Think of it like a shopping trip. You have just seen a dress in a magazine that you absolutely love. You have got a party coming up and you know that this is the dress you want. You venture out shopping and because you know exactly what you want, you focus all your attention on finding the desired item. You are determined to succeed in getting that dress that you are longing for. You see a few other dresses, that are OK, as you wander around the shops but they are not the same as the one that you want. Finally, after a dedicated shopping spree you find the dress that you have been looking for. It is perfect and you are over the moon with your purchase.

However, if you had gone out shopping with no particular purchases in mind, you would probably have come back with things that you didn't really want or need but ended up buying because it was passable and you felt like buying something anyhow.

Knowing exactly what dress you wanted, you didn't give up until you got it. Not knowing what you wanted on other days, you ended up settling for something that was less than perfect for you. This is the same with our relationships. When you know what you want you won't settle for anything less. If you don't have a clear vision of what you are looking for, you'll accept second best.

A relationship is not a possession, it is a process. You don't acquire a relationship, but enter into one 24 hours a day. Know what you want from your relationship. Have a clear vision of the sort of man that you want and the qualities and values he will have. Know exactly how you want your relationship to work, how you will share your love, passion and have fun together. Knowing exactly what you want will allow you to create the right sort of relationship.

- If you are single, create a clear idea of what you want from your relationship.

- If you are in a relationship, knowing what you want will enable you to take your relationship to the next level. If you realise that the relationship you are in is not how you want it, then knowing what you want will give you leverage to clear out what is not right.

Internet dating has become incredibly popular over the last few years because it follows this concept. People state the qualities that they are looking for in a person and the search engine on the site hooks them up with potential suitors. Many of my friends and clients have met their partners on dating sites. My sister met her husband and I met my fiancé using this method, by declaring what we wanted from a man and having a vision of the relationship that we wanted.

Have Positive Beliefs about Relationships

Change any negative beliefs you have about relationships. Believe that you can have the relationship you want.

We all have mixed feelings about relationships at some point in our lives. We all experience good and bad relationships either directly with our own partners or by seeing, hearing and feeling the pain or joy of our friends' relationships. We constantly watch relationships on our TV screens and the cinema. We hear about them on the radio, read about them in books, magazines, papers and experience them all around us. Even when you are sitting on a train, out shopping, having a coffee in the park, you will come across relationships. Relationships are everywhere and depending on whether you are surrounded by good relationships or bad ones, this will affect how you feel about them.

Think about this for a minute; if all your friends are moaning that men are idiots, your dad left your mum for another woman, your boyfriend left you because he wanted to be single and you are constantly reading about infidelity in the papers, you will probably come up with the belief that men were cheating b******s and that relationships never last.

However, if all your friends are in fabulous relationships, you are with a fantastic guy, your mum and dad are blissfully in love, you only read the stories about "such and such a star is in love" and you only watch sloppy romance films, you will have a very different belief to that of the person above and will have strong and positive beliefs about love and relationships.

The truth is that you will never have it as clear cut as those two examples, thus you will have mixed associations of relationships because of conflicting references. On the one hand, you might think that having a relationship will be fantastic because you can share your love; on the other hand, you might think that a relationship will cramp your style and you will lose your freedom. The concept of the stag and hen night reflects this perfectly: "your last night of freedom." This saying gives the impression that marriage will kill freedom.

If you are single, maybe you are associating too much pain with relationships. Maybe you have seen too many others upset by relationships and you link bad feelings to these? Or maybe you have been hurt in the past from a previous relationship and once was enough for you! Alternatively, maybe you are single, simply because you choose to be and you are happy!

If you are single but want to be in a relationship, then you too may still have some negative beliefs about relationships. Although you might be ready for a relationship, subconsciously you are worried that you will end up with somebody like a previous partner, or you might get hurt. Maybe you keep meeting guys that you like, but are unsure that they like you, so nothing happens (self doubt again!). Although you think you want to be in a relationship, you have a lot of negative associations linked to them. Perhaps if you are single and you can't find a suitable man, then it is because you have not been clear on the sort of man you want. Get your wish list declared ASAP!

By ridding yourself of limited beliefs about relationships and having a strong belief about what love is for you, you will be able to create exactly this. I believe that if you can imagine what you want to feel and be like, then you will have exactly this. Our brains do not know the difference between imagination and reality. If you keep visualising what you want, your brain will think that you have this and your subconscious mind will find ways to achieve this. The best belief to have about relationships is…. *If I can imagine having a blissful relationship then I will have one.*

Find Mr Right

Check you have got the right partner and if not, readdress your relationship.

This is definitely the million dollar question, "is this person right for me?" We all find ourselves asking this question at some point or other in our lives and how do we really know the answer?

Does he tick all the boxes in your mental check list? By knowing the sort of person that you want, will help you to answer this question. Ask yourself:

1. Does this person have the same values as you? If he values spending his time more down at the pub than with you and this bothers you, then you will never be happy.

2. Does this person stimulate you emotionally, physically, mentally and intellectually?

3. Does this person want to take your relationship to the next stage?

4. Do you draw out the best in each other, making each other feel good about being the person that you are?

Sometimes, we may ask if our partner has the qualities that we want in him and start thinking that this person is not for us. But remember "emotions bring out behaviours".

If you think your partner isn't very loving, then you might find it hard to always be loving towards him. Sometimes, you express your love but other days you feel fed up and rejected and hold back your love, and you find he doesn't respond how you want him to. However, if you consistently show your partner love, then this should invariably bring out similar feelings in him.

If this still isn't what you want, then he may not be right for you. It is important that you tell your man what he needs to do to make you feel loved, and you need to find out what makes him feel loved. The way we demonstrate our love can be dramatically different from how our partner demonstrates his love. Set up from the start how and what makes both of you feel loved.

Setting High Standards & Putting Them First

Learn to put your partner first.

Set high standards for your relationship and put your partner first. This will make you more of a loving person and will make him feel loved. If you can give out your love to another freely, you will always feel warmth in your heart.

Find out what your partner's needs are and he will give you what you want too. Make sure you create trust and respect for each other. Treat him the way you would want to be treated. Speak the truth, say how you feel, share your fears and worries too. Dedicate time for each other where you focus entirely on each other. Listen to what he has to say and if you don't understand something don't start judging him and jumping to conclusions, but ask him what he means. Miscommunication is a huge issue between males and females because we are such different people. Our brains are wired up in different ways and we don't think in the same way. Understanding one another is vital to having a great relationship. If you can step into your partner's shoes, understand him and give him what he needs, you will have a loving partner for life.

When you're unhappy about something and tell your partner about it, make sure he knows what it is you want, to make it right. The majority of people don't like to state what they want but instead expect their partners to know what is wrong. Don't expect your man to read your mind.

Recipe for Success

One of my clients, Sarah, rushed home from work once to cook dinner for her boyfriend, Russell. They had just moved in together. When she got home, Russell was already there and was happily watching television. Sarah started to cook but soon found herself feeling lonely and unhappy in the kitchen, because she wanted Russell to come and talk to her. She didn't want his help, but just wanted his company. During the meal, Sarah found herself criticising Russell at the dinner table because she was still annoyed that he hadn't come into the kitchen earlier, to be with her. So they ended up having an argument.

Later on that evening, Sarah explained that she was upset because she had wanted his company earlier and felt unloved because he chose to watch TV, instead of being with her. Russell gave her a big hug and told her that he had stayed out of the kitchen as he didn't want to get in her way. He told her that if she had said what she wanted he would have gladly gone into the kitchen to be with her. Russell then asked her to simply tell him, from now on, if she wanted his attention.

Luckily their issue was revolved quickly that night. If Sarah had told him from the start what she had wanted, there would have been no need for an argument. Always let your partner know what you want, instead of expecting him to know what you desire.

Keeping Love Alive

Keeping love and passion alive is something that many couples struggle with, as we start taking our partners for granted. We often forget to focus on building our relationships. Make sure that you don't go down this route or you will be very unhappy. Put the time and effort into your relationship so that you keep your love alive. Feelings die, unless you strengthen and work on them.

- Make time for having fun together. Schedule times for pleasurable dates. Think about setting aside one night a week where you spend quality time together.

- Think about giving him a surprise once a month such as a massage, turning up at his football game, sending him a love letter or taking him to the cinema.

- Be passionate. Think passion. Remember, comfortable tracksuits and PJs will not make you, or your partner, feel turned on. Dress up once in a while. Think sexy thoughts, imagine yourself having a sensual night, and it will happen.

- Spend time together doing things socially with friends. Go to the cinema, for a walk, to the gym, shopping, anything you can enjoy together.

- Learn new things together: a language or watch documentaries.

- Nurture each other emotionally. Show him that you care and tell him how you feel.

- Kiss passionately, at least once a day, to keep your love alive.

- When he has done something to please you, praise him immediately and specifically. This builds up trust and love within your relationship.

Exercises to discover what you want from a partner, a relationship and how to improve both.

EXERCISE ONE

Defining What You Want

Write down beneath, how you want your perfect relationship to be. What would it look like? How would it feel? What sort of things would you be saying to each other on a consistent basis?

_____

_____

_____

_____

Write down all of your limited beliefs associated with relationships, such as loss of freedom, being hurt, being bored or that love never lasts.

My limited beliefs about relationships:

_____

_____

_____

_____

How these beliefs have a negative impact on my life:

_____

_____

_____

_____

_____

_____

Write down inspiring beliefs that will support your relationships. For instance, relationships are fun and a place where you can share your love.

_____

_____

_____

_____

_____

_____

_____

EXERCISE TWO

Define the Man You Want

Write down the qualities of the sort of man that you want. If you already have a partner, does he have all of these qualities?

_____

_____

_____

_____

_____

_____

What sort of person do you need to be, to have the man of your dreams? Write down this list of qualities.

_____

_____

_____

_____

_____

Write down what you need to do, for your partner to feel loved? If you don't know – ask him.

_____

_____

_____

_____

_____

What does your partner need to do, for you to feel loved?

_____

_____

_____

_____

Write a list of actions that you can take to improve your current relationship or the next relationship.

_____

_____

_____

_____

_____

_____

EXERCISE THREE

Wonderful Times

Write down all of the wonderful times that you and your partner have shared together. For example, this might be a silly conversation you had whilst walking one day, or a romantic holiday. List at least 15 times that you have enjoyed together. Keep adding to the list, so that you have a great bank of fabulous memories together.

_____

_____

_____

_____

_____

_____

_____

_____

_____

_____

EXERCISE FOUR

Love Letter

Write a love letter to your man, telling him exactly how you feel about him. Tell him what it was that made you fall for him, what you love about him, what you enjoy doing with him, what he does to make you feel special and what times you have enjoyed with him. This will help rekindle your feelings towards him.

What can you do together to have fun and ignite your passion?

_____

_____

_____

_____

_____

_____

💜 What can you do, intimately, that will make him feel loved?

_____

_____

_____

_____

_____

_____

EXERCISE FIVE

Imagine & You Can... Have a Blissful Relationship

Visualisation time for 5 minutes every day

💜 See yourself, in detail, totally happy in a loving and blissful relationship. See yourself like this in everyday life. Be the director of your own movie, where you are the star.

💜 Make the movie as perfect as possible. Imagine yourself in a wonderful relationship, where you are able to share intimate thoughts. See yourself being affectionate with one another and happy. See yourself having fun and laughing. Hear the kind and loving words you share with one another. Feel how good it is when you are in love and you are holding one another and looking into each other's eyes.

💜 Once you are satisfied, see yourself in the picture and imagine doing it for real. See what you would see if you had a blissful and loving relationship, hear what you would hear and notice how you respond to each other.

When you are happy with your movie, store it away in your own personal DVD collection in your mind, knowing you can see it at any time.

EXERCISE SIX

Changing Roles for Five Minutes

Practise every day for seven days stepping into either your partner's shoes, or if you do not have a partner, then somebody that you like. Walk, talk and behave how they would, so you can start to understand other people's perspectives more. This will enable you to understand others more easily and how they feel. It will allow you to be more flexible in your relationships.

EXERCISE SEVEN

Self-Coaching

Use this self-coaching session to improve your relationship. If you are not in a relationship, then still carry out this session, but instead think about how you want your next relationship to be and how to get this.

G is for Goal

(On a scale of 1-10, where 1 is not at all and 10 is completely happy)

💜 How happy am I with my relationship? _____

💜 What do I need to do to make it a 10?

_____

_____

_____

_____

_____

💜 Think about having the most perfect relationship and take yourself forward to a point in time where you have this. What do you notice that shows that you have this perfect relationship? How do you know this has happened?

_____

_____

_____

_____

_____

💜 What are you doing that shows you that you have this blissful relationship? Make a quick note.

_____

_____

_____

_____

_____

❤ What are you hearing that tells you that your relationship is wonderfully happy?

_____

_____

_____

_____

❤ How are you feeling at this point in the future?

_____

_____

_____

_____

❤ What are you saying to yourself?

_____

_____

_____

_____

❤ How will you know that you have this blissful relationship? Is there a measurement you can use?

_____

_____

_____

_____

R is for Reality

❤ What is going on now that tells you that you don't have a blissful relationship?

_____

_____

_____

_____

❤ What have you done, so far, to improve things?

_____

_____

_____

_____

_____

_____

❤ What were the obstacles you met from doing these things?

_____

_____

_____

_____

_____

_____

❤ What do you need to do, to help you to achieve this blissful relationship?

_____

_____

_____

_____

_____

_____

❤ Are there any resources that might help you to achieve this blissful relationship?

_____

_____

_____

_____

_____

O is for Options

Now that we have clarified the minute details of a blissful relationship, let's consider the options available to you.

❤ What could you do to move yourself one step forward to get this blissful relationship?

_____

_____

_____

❤ Write down as many ways you can think of, to achieve your blissful relationship?

_____

_____

_____

_____

❤ If you went to your guardian angel for help to improve your relationship, what might she suggest?

_____

_____

_____

_____

❤ If money was unlimited what could you do, in order to achieve this relationship?

_____

_____

_____

_____

❤ If you secretly knew what you should do first, what would it be?

_____

_____

❤ Choose one of the previous options that you think would be right for you to do now. Circle it. If you do this, will it move you forward? If not, choose something else.

❤ How will this option make your relationship more blissful?

_____

_____

_____

W is for Will

❤ What are you going to do?

_____

_____

_____

_____

❤ How will these actions allow you to have this blissful relationship?

_____

_____

_____

❤ When are you going to take these actions?

_____

_____

❤ Should anybody else be involved in this list of actions?

_____

_____

_____

❤ What do you want this person, or these people to do?

_____

_____

_____

♥ When will you tell them?

_____

_____

_____

♥ Who else should know that you are doing these things?

_____

_____

_____

♥ When will you tell them?

_____

_____

_____

♥ Whatever your first step is, can you think of any obstacle that might stop you from doing it?

_____

_____

_____

♥ How likely is it to stop you? If likely, what can you do to make your first step more achievable?

_____

_____

_____

♥ Who will help you to overcome this obstacle?

_____

_____

_____

❤ What will you do to stop it from stopping you?

_____

_____

_____

_____

_____

❤ Is there anything else you need to consider before you begin?

_____

_____

_____

_____

_____

❤ On a scale of 1-10, where 10 is "I am totally committed to having a blissful relationship and taking action", where are you?

_____

_____

_____

❤ If you are not a 10 – what do you need to do to make it a 10?

_____

_____

_____

_____

_____

Chapter Eight

Be Caring
& Help Others

To be caring or not to be caring,
that is the question.

Caring: a feeling of concern, interest,
affection, liking, consideration.

In this Chapter you will:

- Learn how to be more caring

- Discover how to become a 'better listener'

- Find out ways of helping others in your community

- Find out strategies for making your loved ones feel more loved

Be Caring

Do you want to feel fulfilled every day of your life? Do you want to be someone whom others love to be around, someone that touches others' lives and makes a difference to this world? Do you want to wake up every day and be proud of who you are? Then you need to be caring. Use your greatest gift in life – your heart – to light up all those around you and help make the world a better place. Caring for and giving to those around you will not only make you a better person, but you will feel very happy knowing that you are making a positive difference to others.

This chapter will show you the magic that you can create in your life by being a caring and sharing person. Being caring and giving is not just about charity work and donating money but also about giving your time and energy to others. Learn the ultimate tool for being caring which is how to listen properly and make someone feel wonderful. More importantly, discover the art of self-fulfilment.

The purpose of *Imagine & You Can* is to help you to achieve more of the good feelings in life. Being caring is definitely one of my favourite feelings. At first, you might not think that this is a feeling that most of us strive for. But you'd be wrong!

We are constantly bombarded with information from the media on how to be more healthy, happy, confident or motivated. Everywhere you look there is advice and tips on how to have better relationships and increase your self-love, more and more press coverage on the merits of gratitude and visualisation, a mass of information on personal development and numerous books and articles on how to have more fun and passion in your life. But do you ever see information on being a more caring person?

Fortunately, being caring is natural for many of us, as the large number of charities in the world shows (over 170,000 in the UK alone). People want to feel good in themselves and do this by the unselfish act of giving and helping others. Caring makes you feel fantastically alive. Knowing you are helping others, in turn helps you to feel warm and wonderful inside.

Remember: when you leave this world, people will not remember you for what you had, but for who you were – a caring and loving soul

When I was teenager, I was a taker. I didn't realise it at the time, but I often used people to help me to feel better about myself. I hate to admit that I was like this, but it is true. I used to think about how such and such a person could help me, or what they could do for me. Looking back on it now, I have realised that I was someone that gave gifts or help to others just so that I could get something in return. I told myself that this was acceptable but it wasn't, because ultimately it didn't make me happy.

As a teenager, I loved receiving attention from guys. I used to play the role of a damsel in distress, so that my boyfriend or male friends looked after me and would do all they could for me. I was terrible for doing this and relied heavily on guys to run around after me. At the time, I couldn't see a problem in my behaviour. Yet, even with all this attention, I never felt truly happy. For years, I couldn't understand why I felt empty. I constantly searched for ways to feel good about myself through others but it never worked. I expected others to make me happy without my reciprocating their affection.

It took me many years to realise that I can't expect other people to make me happy. People need to make their own happiness. Taking from other people all the time will never fulfil anyone. To be fulfilled, you need to be caring and give your love to others. The act of kindness is what fulfils us and makes our spirit come alive.

If you know what you are doing for others is making a difference and having a positive impact on their lives, you will keep doing it. When you start to become caring and experience how great it feels, you will never go back to being a taker. Think of Ebeneezer Scrooge in Dickens' classic "A Christmas Carol." When he finally stopped being a miser and started to give to those needy people around him, he was happy and fulfilled instead of being miserable and lonely.

Would you classify yourself as a giver or a taker? A giver is somebody who gives their time, their love, their energy and maybe their money to others. A taker is, of course, somebody who does the opposite. Which feels better to you?

Caring for Friends and Family

How do you show your friends and family that you care? By giving them affection through the power of touch? By listening to them and trying to understand them? By saying nice words to soothe them? By being considerate and taking action to make their lives easier, such as by doing some cooking or cleaning for them? By buying gifts for them so they know you've thought about them?

There are lots of different ways to show someone that you care and we all have different strategies to do so. There is no right or wrong way and the secret to it is to know what makes that person feel special.

When a friend of mine broke up with her boyfriend and was devastated, I went round to her house, gave her a big hug, and listened to her for hours. But I also bought her some flowers and some of her favourite chocolates and she told me the next day that was what had made her feel loved and cared for. She needed to cry on my shoulder but her own way of making someone feel special was to buy them a gift, so when I had done that for her, she knew that I cared.

We all have different ways of letting someone know that we care. Also, we all have different ways of feeling special ourselves, whether that is by getting a present, like my friend, being hugged, being listened to, being cuddled, being distracted... Ask your friends and family what makes them feel special. And if you don't know, make the effort of doing whatever you can.

Listening

An important way to show someone that you care is by giving them your quality time, where you focus on them entirely and listen properly. Giving somebody 100% of your attention will make them feel special and loved.

When you pay close attention to another individual and actively listen to what they have to say, you will make them feel like the most important person in the world. As someone once said to me, "You have two ears and one mouth, so use them in that proportion." Listening is crucial in caring for others but it is also something that many of us are very bad at. We assume that once we start to speak to the person we are with, they will automatically start to listen. But this is not the case, as the level that they choose to listen to us could range from not at all to very attentive.

How irritated do you feel when you have been talking to your friends and think they are listening, only to find later when you talk to them about the same subject, that they clearly weren't? It makes you feel like they don't care. So many of us are terrible listeners. It is crucial that we have this skill, to fully understand and connect with our loved ones. When we don't feel understood by others, we feel alone and separated. You can't be understood by someone until they listen to you wholeheartedly.

Listening is not an easy skill and something you need to practise

Every one of us has our own opinions, beliefs and values and it is very easy as a listener to interpret the speaker's words according to your own views. It is all too easy to stop our friend in mid-flow and give our opinion, hence not listening to what she has to say. When you're listening to someone and they start talking about an event or an experience and you recognise a similar situation that you have been in, you automatically start listening in terms of your own experience, or wait for a chance to interrupt and tell them about it, and so you don't really listen to, or understand their experience.

How you feel at any given moment will also have a dramatic impact on your listening skills. If you are feeling happy and optimistic, you will pick up on the positive things that your friends have to say. If you are feeling a bit depressed or bored, then you will tend to focus on the negative parts of what is being said. The way that you listen is affected by your emotions. You must put your moods on hold when you are listening to others.

Listening is not an easy skill and something you need to practise. When you are able to listen to others properly, you can satisfy their needs and wants more easily. Consequently, you will have a far better relationship with someone because you understand them better. When people are listened to, they feel that they matter, and what they think and feel is important. This builds a solid foundation between two people and displays encouragement and support.

TIPS FOR LISTENING

💜 Maintain good eye contact

💜 Lean slightly towards the speaker

💜 Concentrate on them

💜 Keep an open mind – even if you disagree with what is being said. Listen to them and don't change the subject

💜 Don't interrupt somebody unless it is to clarify a point by asking questions

💜 Move away from external distractions

💜 Leave your own feelings behind

💜 Be patient, allow them to speak

💜 Show the talker that you want to listen and that you care

💜 Try to understand them better, by putting yourself in their shoes

---

Do you think you're as caring and as sharing as you could be with your family, friends and partner? Do you think that you listen to them effectively and understand them fully? What actions do you need to take now, to demonstrate that you care about your loved ones?

Outside Your Social Circle

Caring and helping those we love is a great way of improving our own personal relationships. But what about giving to people that we don't know? Do you give your time or money to strangers? Have you ever done this? Would you ever do this?

At my primary school, we were taught to think about others who were less fortunate and how we could help them. Around harvest time every year, we collected tins of food from home to take to school and make food parcels, to give to the elderly. The teachers told us at the time how much this food would make a difference to these people's lives, as many of them didn't have much money for food or were immobile and so couldn't go shopping easily. To this day, I still remember how good it felt handing over our parcels to the old people whom we visited and seeing them smile. There are so many people much worse off than us and doing small things to help them will make a difference.

Imagine This

Imagine yourself at the end of your life. You are 95, in a bed-sit, all on your own. You are sitting in a worn out armchair on a threadbare carpet with only a TV in the room for company. Your partner is dead and you have no other family or friends. You are incredibly lonely. You are huddled up in a chair watching the TV, wearing layers of old clothes to try to keep yourself warm. You can't afford to put the heating on. You wonder whether you will ever have another visitor. You haven't eaten all day because you are trying to make your food last.

Suddenly your doorbell rings. You manage to get up and hobble to the front door wondering whether you have forgotten to pay the milkman the other day, and if so, can you afford to pay him? You open the door slightly with the latch on, so you can close it quickly, if it is a stranger. There in front of you is a young woman holding a brightly coloured box with four small children smiling at you.

The woman explains that she is a teacher and has come to visit you with her primary school students, to give you a gift of food for the harvest festival. You are overjoyed. You are touched that these young people have come here to not only give you some very much needed food, but to give you some of their time. You let them in. The children are happy and giggly and chat away to you. You feel the warmth from their souls and they light up the room with their energy. When the children have gone, you realise that although you do not have any company there with you in your bed-sit, you are never alone as others do still care.

We must remember that many others are worse off than us. Remember, we all get old and one day it might be you who is lonely and has nobody to talk to. Think about acts of kindness that you can do.

Your Time

Give up some of your free time, even if it is just an hour a month, to do some charity work and help others. If you are an animal lover, contact charities such as The Blue Cross and donate some of your time to go into schools and teach small children how to look after their pets. Help terminally ill people by giving up some of your time to do voluntary work in hospices. Do some community work or help to change the attitudes of others. There are many charity websites that will put you in contact with those that you can help. One of the best that I recently discovered was **www.vinspired.com**. By telling the website what you're looking for and where you want to work, the search engine on this site will seek out opportunities that are right for you, allowing you to use your passions, skills and talents to the advantage of others.

Contributions of Money

As children, it's unlikely that we will donate our pocket money to charity. When we start earning our first wage, it is often difficult for us to contribute some of this, as we are in debt from university or we are starting out and every penny counts. So when is the right time to give to charity? When we are earning lots and life is comfortable? When we win the lottery? There is no rule whether you do or you don't contribute money. However, is there ever a good time to give your money to charity? Even if you are rich, you will always find ways of spending your money and will find yourself still wanting a car or a new house, just the next level up.

Why should you want to give your money to charity? Because you know even if you are having a bad day, you have PMT and have been an absolute "cow", you are still doing some good in the world by giving. You have the inner knowledge that you are doing some good in the world and are still a caring human being with a wonderful spirit and heart.

The Quick Fix Contribution

A smile or a small gesture of kindness, such as helping an elderly or a blind person across the road, can make someone's day. Has a complete stranger, for no apparent reason, ever smiled or said 'hello' to you? Did it brighten up your life for a brief moment? All those moments add up. When was the last time that you walked down the road, smiled and said 'hello' to a complete stranger? You will never know the effect this could have on someone.

Gestures

I recently received an email with a story attached to it about how one small gesture changed a person's life. I will now paraphrase this story for you. Hopefully, it will touch your soul as it did mine and show you the power of being caring.

Charlotte was walking home from school one Friday, when she saw another girl from her year, Rebecca, shuffling along the road carrying a mass of books. "Why would anyone bring home all her books on a Friday?" Charlotte thought. "She must be a nerd." She shrugged her shoulders and walked on.

As she was walking, Charlotte saw a bunch of kids run towards Rebecca. They knocked all the books out of her arms and tripped her up, so that she landed in the dirt. Her glasses went flying and landed in the grass.

Rebecca looked up and Charlotte saw a terrible sadness in her eyes. Her heart went out to Rebecca, so she jogged over to her. She handed Rebecca her glasses and said, "Those kids are jerks. Are you all right?" She helped Rebecca pick up the books and asked her where she lived. They got talking, and Charlotte asked her if she wanted to hang out with her and her friends that weekend. She had a busy weekend planned with parties and a DVD watching session. Rebecca said 'yes'.

The two girls became best friends over the next few years, only being separated when Rebecca went to university, in the States, to train as a doctor. But they remained close, and when Rebecca graduated, Charlotte flew to the States to hear Rebecca's graduation speech.

Rebecca was nervous about the speech, but Charlotte calmed her down and encouraged her, just as she had on the day that they had first met. Rebecca started speaking. She said:

"Graduation is a time to thank all those who helped you through those tough years. Our parents, siblings, teachers, maybe a coach, but mostly our friends. I am here to tell all of you that being a friend to someone is the best gift you can give them. I am going to tell you a story."

Charlotte looked at her friend in disbelief as she told the story of the first day they met. Rebecca had been planning to kill herself that weekend. She had cleaned out her locker so her mum wouldn't have to do it later and was carrying all of her stuff home.

Rebecca looked at Charlotte and gave her a smile. "Thankfully, I was saved," she said. "My friend saved me from doing the unspeakable. I am so grateful for her helping me that day."

There were gasps in the crowd as this beautiful and clever girl shared her story about her weakest moment. Charlotte was shocked too, as it wasn't until then that she realised how that one small gesture of hers had changed her friend's life. And who knows, maybe even Rebecca's bravery in sharing that story gave hope to someone in the audience who heard it.

When I read this story it reinforced the importance to me about considering and caring for others, even in the tiniest of ways. Even the smallest action can make such a difference to someone's life. Never underestimate the power of your actions. Look out for other people, and be caring to everyone around you. Your acts of kindness will make a difference to other people's lives. There is nothing more fulfilling than bringing joy to another person.

❤ ❤

EXERCISE ONE

Listening & Giving Your Attention

Get into the habit of listening to people fully with both ears and with no distractions. Practise doing this. Every day over the next week, remind yourself that you have to listen to the person whom you are with. If you find yourself not listening, then tell yourself to stop whatever you are doing or thinking about and focus on this person. Try for a whole week to not interrupt whoever you are with and only say something back when they have stopped talking. Score yourself daily on how many times you interrupt somebody.

EXERCISE TWO

Smiling & Kind Gestures

Over the next week, set yourself a goal to smile and say "hello" to a stranger every day. Each day, increase how many strangers you greet and increase your smiles and kind gestures.

By doing this daily, you will find after a week or two that it is natural for you to say "hello" and smile at others, thereby making others feel good. And of course, yourself!

EXERCISE THREE

Eliciting Strategies

❤ Ask your loved ones what you need to do to make them feel special and loved.

❤ Ask them whether you need to give them more affection.

❤ Ask them if you need to say kind words more.

❤ Ask them whether you need to buy or make them presents.

❤ Ask them what you can do to show them how much you care.

EXERCISE FOUR

Hour of Time

Over the next week, think about what you could do for others by means of voluntary work.

Have a look at www.vinspired.com and see what there is available that you can do and enjoy. Committing to doing something for others will make you feel wonderful about yourself.

EXERCISE FIVE

Record When You Give

To understand how you feel when you are charitable, keep a record for a week and write down the occasions when you have given to someone and how it felt afterwards. How generous have you been this week? Try to increase it next week.

_____

_____

_____

_____

EXERCISE SIX

Money For Others

Decide what you are willing to give to others and do it.

Questions

💜 How will it affect my relationships by listening to others properly and giving them my time and attention?

_____

_____

_____

💜 If I don't properly listen to others, how does that make them feel?

_____

_____

_____

💜 How will it make others feel by smiling and saying "hello" to them in the street? How will it make me feel?

_____

_____

_____

💜 How will volunteering an hour of my time to charities have an impact on others?

_____

_____

💜 What will being more of a giver and less of a taker do for my self-esteem?

_____

_____

💜 How will giving money to people, who are far worse off than me, improve their lives?

_____

_____

_____

Self-Coaching

To be a better person you need to be more caring about others. Self–coach yourself on how to be more caring and giving to others, so that you feel even better about yourself.

The self coaching session will take about 30-45 minutes.

G is for Goal

(On a scale of 1-10, where 1 is "not at all" and 10 is "completely happy")

💜 How much do I help others? _____

💜 What would make it a 10?

_____

_____

💜 Think about being caring and take yourself forward to a point in time when you are at your most compassionate. What do you notice that shows you that you are now like this? Or how do you know that this has happened?

_____

_____

_____

💜 What are you doing that shows you that you are caring to others?

_____

_____

_____

💜 What are you hearing that tells you that you are caring to others?

_____

_____

_____

💜 How are you feeling at this point in the future?

_____

_____

💜 What are you saying to yourself?

_____

_____

R is for Reality

💜 What is going on right now that tells you that you don't care enough about others and don't give enough to others?

_____

_____

💜 What have you done so far to improve things?

_____

_____

_____

💜 What were the obstacles you met when doing these things?

_____

_____

_____

❤ What obstacles or possible barriers are in your way that prevent or hinder you from moving forwards?

_____

_____

_____

❤ What do you need to do to help you to be more caring?

_____

_____

_____

❤ Are there any resources that might help you to be more caring and to give to others?

_____

_____

_____

O is for Options

Now we are going to explore the sort of actions that you can take to be caring and giving.

❤ What could you do to move yourself just one step forward now?

_____

_____

_____

❤ Go wild and write down as many ways that you can think of to be more caring and sharing to your friends, family, partner, strangers and people who are worse off than you.

_____

_____

_____

_____

❤ What else could you do if you didn't have to explain what you were doing or be answerable to anybody?

_____

_____

_____

❤ If you could devote all your time to being caring and giving to others, what would you do then?

_____

_____

_____

❤ If you went to your guardian angel for help so that you could be more caring and be able to give more, what might she suggest?

_____

_____

❤ What could you do, if money was unlimited, to help others more?

_____

_____

_____

❤ If you secretly know what you should do first, what would it be?

_____

_____

❤ Choose one of the options that you think would be right for you to do now. Circle it. If you do the one thing that you have chosen, will it move you forward? If not choose something else.

❤ How will this option make you more caring and helpful to others?

_____

_____

_____

W is for Will

♥ What will you do? List the actions so that you now start to give more to others and thus show your caring side?

_____

_____

_____

_____

♥ How will these actions allow you to be more caring to others?

_____

_____

♥ When are you going to take these actions?

_____

_____

♥ Should anybody else be involved in this list of actions?

_____

_____

_____

♥ What do you want this person, or these people to do?

_____

_____

♥ When will you tell them?

_____

_____

♥ Who else should know that you are doing these things?

_____

_____

💜 When will you tell them?

_____

_____

💜 Whatever your first step is, can you think of any obstacle that might stop you from doing it?

_____

_____

💜 How likely is it to stop you? If likely, what can you do to make your first step more achievable?

_____

_____

💜 How will you overcome this obstacle?

_____

_____

💜 What will you do, to stop it from stopping you?

_____

_____

_____

💜 Is there anything else you need to consider before you begin?

_____

_____

💜 On a scale of 1-10 where 10, is "I am totally committed to being more caring, giving to others and taking action", where are you?

_____

💜 If you are not a 10 – what do you need to do to make it a 10?

_____

_____

Chapter Nine

Have Outstanding Health & Wellbeing

To be healthy or not to be healthy,
that is the question.

Healthy: not unwell or diseased but normal,
well, fine and fit, in body and mind.

In this Chapter you will:

- Learn how to have outstanding health
- Discover how to alkalise your body and always feel fabulous
- Find out how to eat and exercise sensibly
- Find out to how to be balanced with fantastic 'wellbeing'

> *I believe that this is the MOST IMPORTANT CHAPTER in the book*
> *and so I saved the best till last!*

Feeling Healthy

In my opinion, feeling healthy is the most important feeling in the world. When you are unhealthy you have little energy, you feel uninspired with your life and you feel unhappy. Having great health determines how great you feel.

When you have excellent health you have an abundance of vitality and energy, making you live life to the full. Having outstanding health needs to be a priority for you if you want to live your life to the full, every day. Equally, having a profound sense of wellbeing is also important. Wellbeing means being physically, emotionally and mentally fit. When you have outstanding health and wellbeing you will live a life full of energy, happiness and fulfilment. Your life is in balance and you feel wonderful.

Being healthy and having a body that you feel proud of makes you feel fantastic inside and look fabulous on the outside. When you look after yourself your self-esteem is much higher, giving you a more positive attitude and approach to life. People with high self-esteem are far more likely to be proactive in their lives and make things happen because they believe in themselves.

If you allow yourself to become overweight, unhealthy and unfit you will naturally start to feel unhappy because you are not treating yourself with the respect you deserve.

Look after your health and wellbeing. Nurture yourself. Set yourself high standards so that every day you have an abundance of energy.

How many days in your life have you not had the energy to do things you wanted to, such as exercise, socialising with friends, shopping or making love with your partner? Most people deplete themselves of energy by rushing around and create stress by thinking negatively and living an unhealthy lifestyle.

As soon as you become healthier, your energy levels increase and you will have the energy to invest in your relationships, your work life, your friends, family and your own wellbeing.

The power of your health and wellbeing cannot be underestimated. By working on these areas you will transform your life dramatically.

How We Get Unhealthy

Health and wellbeing is not usually an issue when you are young, unless you have some specific health challenges. In fact, the issue of health is not high on our priority list until we start to get older and see our health and energy levels decline.

As teenagers and young adults many of us are more concerned about being skinny, like WAGS and celebrities, than being healthy. Body image seems to count for everything and unfortunately many of the eating habits and lifestyle choices, that young people follow to get thin, drastically affect their state of health and wellbeing. Something has to give and this will be your health, as well as your emotional and mental wellbeing.

During the period of our lives when we must work for a living, many of us are more concerned about creating wealth and think very little about our health. The pressure of looking good, in a materialistic world, does not allow us much time to focus on strengthening our emotional and physical health.

Having a balanced life is vital to your happiness.

We put constant pressure on ourselves to earn more money and have bigger and better things, but while we are working day and night to get the lifestyle we want, we forget about looking after ourselves. Often we neglect exercising, as we don't have the time nor energy and we eat fast foods because they are quick after a long day's work. Finally, this catches up with us and one day we wake up, wondering why we're so unhappy and why we're feeling run down all the time. We start to notice we don't have the energy that we want and the body we deserve. Does this sound familiar?

Having a balanced life is vital to your happiness. There is nothing wrong with working hard but remember to give yourself time to relax too.

One of the biggest gifts we can give ourselves is time. Time to relax, time to unwind from the pressures of life, time with loved ones, time to exercise, time to have fun, time to have a hobby, time to buy and cook the right foods and time to look after ourselves, so that we are physically, mentally and emotionally fit.

Live a peaceful life. Stress depletes you of energy and your spirit. Put your health and wellbeing above all else. Give yourself the gift of time and commit to having outstanding health and wellbeing. If you don't have this, then it will be very difficult for you to enjoy your life. You need to be emotionally, mentally and physically fit to have outstanding health and wellbeing. This means you need to nurture all three areas to ensure you feel and look fabulous at all times.

Being happy and having positive feelings affects your biochemistry and thus your state of health and wellbeing. There have been numerous studies over the years to show how the mind and body are inextricably linked and that how you feel emotionally determines how you feel physically. A happy and balanced person stimulates their immune system, whilst a depressed person literally depresses their immune system and can cause himself or herself ill-health.

The mind has immense power over the body. People who have been incredibly ill, with awful diseases and not expected to live, have defied the odds by adopting a positive mindset. The power of the mind and having faith is something that can't be dismissed.

Having a positive state of mind will help you to stay healthy. Being continually stressed and having negative thoughts can cause you to become ill and lead to many health problems.

Make your Mind up to be Healthy & Happy

Your mind can make you healthy or sick. A depressed immune system is created by stress, and this is caused by your state of mind. Cure yourself by laughter therapy. Laughter and a good positive state of mind will stimulate your immune system and will help you to have good wellbeing.

Direct yourself back to good health with a powerful mind that is full of hope, love, faith, purpose, playfulness, determination and passion. Have positive thoughts and emotions to keep you in fantastic condition. Your thoughts affect how you feel instantaneously and can improve your health dramatically.

Imagine Yourself as Healthy

What do you need to do to feel and be healthy? Imagine you are at the peak of health and you feel wonderful and full of energy. You wake up in the morning and instead of rolling back over to sleep, you jump out of bed bursting with energy. During the day, your energy levels remain high and constant so that you feel great all day, no matter what. After your day's work, still raring to go, you do an hour's session at the gym. Then to end your day, you catch up with your friends and family – still feeling refreshed. You feel motivated and alive. Have you ever felt like that?

Most people don't have the energy levels they want. They feel exhausted by the afternoon and can't muster the energy to do much after work except to sit in front of the TV, in a daze. Most people accept this as being normal, but it doesn't have to be. If you want to increase your energy levels, then you can.

What do you need to do to consistently feel 100% healthy and full of energy? If you had to score your health out of 10, where 10 is "fantastic and the picture of health", where would you be? Where would you like to be? 10? I hope so. *Imagine & You Can...*

The first thing you need to start looking at is living a healthy lifestyle. I have been working in the health and fitness industry for the last ten years and I am passionate about how important this is. Health and wellbeing is not just about exercising and eating the right nutrition, it is about keeping your body in balance. So let's uncover the guiding fundamentals to staying healthy.

What do you associate with having good health? For most people, when they suddenly decide to become healthier, they look at changing their diet first and then exercise. This is good, as the right food is very important. But it is not the main concern when considering health. The simple fact is: we can go without food for months, without water for a few days, yet we can only be without oxygen for a few minutes. *This means that oxygen is the most important factor for us, in order to be healthy and alive.*

Now you might be sitting there, thinking, "Excellent, I breathe already so I don't have a problem." Wrong!

The problem is that most of us are not breathing properly. We are not getting enough oxygen around our bodies for our cells to work efficiently and create the energy we need, and so we feel tired.

Good breathing is vital for us to cleanse our lymph/immune system. If our lymph system isn't getting the oxygen it needs, it won't be able to do its job sufficiently of eliminating toxins. The toxins then start to build up and we feel tired and sluggish. Severe toxicity in our bodies makes us ill and can cause all sorts of diseases. Taking deep diaphramic breaths is the first step in helping us to feel more alive and full of energy.

INCREASING OXYGEN FLOW

How to Breathe Properly to Feel Healthy

- Place your hand on your stomach. Breathe as you normally would, and notice whether your hand and stomach rise and fall, or your chest rises and falls, as you breathe. When you breathe properly your chest will stay still while your stomach will rise slightly as you breathe in. While you breathe out, your chest will continue to stay still, while your stomach lowers slightly.

- Now slowly take a deep breath in through your nose on the count of five while gently pushing down on your stomach. Feel the lungs expanding with air.

- Hold the breath for a count of five seconds so that the body is really enriched with oxygen

- Slowly exhale through your mouth for a count of five, while gently pushing down on your stomach.

- Do a set of ten breaths, three to five times a day, to increase your oxygen levels.

- Whenever you are tired, do a set of ten deep breaths to get your oxygen and blood flow circulating more effectively.

Energise Yourself with Water

Water is an essential and major element of all living matter, and the largest single component of our bodies. Water is the one substance (other than oxygen) that we must absolutely have if we are to stay healthy. Your body needs water to function properly. When we don't have enough water, we feel tired and become sick. When we have no water, we die.

Approximately 70% of your body is made up of water. Ideally, 70% of your diet also needs to be made up of water-rich foods, as this will allow your body to cleanse itself and flush out any toxins, stopping you from becoming unhealthy. Water rich foods are living foods not processed or packaged. Any fruit, salad and vegetables are rich in water.

It seems that most people I know probably only have a diet that is made up of 25% water. No wonder people feel run down and depleted of energy! Many of us don't even drink water. Instead we have fruit juice, fizzy drinks, tea, coffee and alcohol. While these are all liquids, they are not substitutes for water, as they are full of sugars or caffeine which are toxic to your body.

So how much water is in your diet? Write down everything that you eat and drink today on a piece of paper and calculate approximately the percentage of water you have daily from food and drink.

Breakfast: _____

_____

(Remember coffee, tea, fruit juice, and milk do not count as water. Cereal, toast and fry-ups don't have water in them either. But fruit does!)

Lunch: _____

_____

_____

Dinner: _____

_____

_____

Snacks: _____

_____

(Pasta, rice, meat, cheese, yoghurt, chicken, fish and so on are not classed as water rich foods. Only your salads and vegetables.)

I remember the first time I realised how little water-rich foods I had. It shocked me. Since having nearly 70% of my diet made up of waters, I have noticed a considerable difference to my health and wellbeing. I feel more energetic, my blood sugar seems to be more balanced and I feel far happier because I know I am looking after myself in the best possible way. I know there are lots of tasty foods available, but unfortunately most of them block our systems and don't stimulate our body and mind naturally. Chocolate and coffee have often been referred to as an energy-giving stimulant. They might give you energy superficially but deep within your body, they are causing havoc to your blood sugars and are no good for you.

If you can increase the amount of water in your diet you will naturally stimulate yourself with vital energy.

Learn to recognize and identify the signs of dehydration. Learn how to hydrate properly and what kind of waters to use for maximum health benefits. There are many different kinds of water available, such as tap water, mountain spring, distilled or carbonated water. Some of the bottled water and tap water have chemicals and impurities in them, so filter your water before drinking it.

SIMPLE STEPS TO TAKE NOW:

- Drink 2-3 litres of water a day

- Have as much food with live waters in them. Water is in vegetables, (especially dark green leafy vegetables), salads and fruit.

- To increase the amount of water rich foods that you have, aim to have three-quarters of your meals as vegetables or salad.

A Slightly Alkaline Body is Crucial for Good Health & Energy

Have you ever been into the chemist and seen those PH strips to wee on and see how acidic your body is? I highly recommend doing this, so you can test your acidity levels.

Your blood needs to have a PH level of 7.36, which is slightly alkaline, to maintain good health. If it isn't alkaline, in other words if it is acidic, then you will have an acidic atmosphere in your body and you will feel low in energy. We need to alkalise our bodies as much as possible, to help break down the cycle of excess acid in our bodies. Acid is created very easily in our bodies and it is vital that we know what causes it, so that we can try to minimise it. We also need to know how to alkalise our bodies to stay healthy.

What Causes an Acidic Environment?

💜 **Negative Emotions** - Thoughts, words and actions all have a vast impact on your bloodstream. Have you ever had that churning feeling inside your stomach when you are nervous or stressed? It's caused by excess acid, which is brought on by your emotions. Many of us will experience bad emotions sometimes but if you are someone who constantly moans, feels angry, jealous, bitter, frustrated, anxious, upset, worried or depressed then you need to make changes now.

- 💜 Go for quiet walks and get back to nature to help you unwind

- 💜 Take some form of exercise to help increase your endorphins

- 💜 Read self help books to help you overcome your negativity

- 💜 Have some NLP therapy or coaching

- 💜 Watch funny films and spend time with young children

Ask yourself before you do anything from now on -

"Will this make me feel better about myself?"

This is a great question to ask and will help you to come up with better choices for living your life.

💜 **An Acid Diet** - Tea, coffee, fizzy drinks, sugar, a high fatty diet, cooked oils, animal proteins and refined carbohydrates all create large amounts of acid in your body.

Unfortunately, too much of any food group, except vegetables and salads, can have a detrimental affect on your health and could also be a reason why you might find it hard to lose excess fat or body weight.

Too Much Acid Could Be Why You Are Over Weight

Acid formation is a large factor for underlying fat retention and weight gain. Fat storage is one of the body's ways of protecting the inner organs from the destructive and corrosive effect of excess acid in your blood. As soon as you start alkalizing your body, you will automatically find that your excess body fat drops off and your energy levels soar. Try to eat more alkalising foods from the list below and cut down on your acid forming foods to feel and see the benefits of an alkalising food regime. When you do eat acid forming foods, make sure you counter balance this with large portions of vegetables or salad which are our alkalising foods. Aim to have at least 70% of the food on your plate made up of greens!

When you start eating more green foods and start to feel fantastic and full of energy, you will never go back to a diet of junk food.

ALKALISING FOODS
(Aim to make up 70% of your diet with these foods)

- **Vegetables** – Especially good are asparagus, artichokes, lettuce, onions, cauliflower, radish, swede, peas, courgettes, red cabbage, wheat grass, watercress, chives, leeks, cabbage, cucumber, broccoli, green beans, beetroot, celery, garlic, brussel sprouts, spinach, carrots, turnips, yams and dandelion.

- **Fruits** – Tomatoes, limes, lemons, avocados, grapefruits, bananas, sour cherries, coconut and figs. Watermelon is neutral.

- **Nuts** – Almonds, brazil nuts and pine nuts.

- **Seeds** – Sunflower, sesame, flax, caraway, pumpkin, barley, cumin, and fennel.

- **Grains** – Soy flour, millet, buckwheat, spelt, lentils, lima beans, fresh soy beans, basmati rice, jasmine rice, fresh soya beans, bulgur, couscous, oats, rye bread and tofu.

- **Fats & Oils** – Flax, hemp, avocado, borage, primrose, olive, coconut, sesame oil, oil blends such as Udo's choice.

- **Fish** – Cold water fish rich in omega 3, mackerel, trout, cod, tuna, fresh salmon and halibut.

- **Beverages** – Water, lemon water, non sweetened soy milk, almond milk, herbal tea, vegetable juice or wheatgrass super green powder drink!

ACID FORMING FOODS
(Aim to have a maximum of 30% of these foods in your diet)

- **Roots** - Potatoes

- **Fruits** – All except those under Alkalising foods. Still eat some acidic forming fruit, but in moderation!

- **Nuts** – Peanuts, cashew nuts, filberts, hazelnuts, macadamia nuts, walnuts and pistachio nuts.

- **Grains** – Wheat grain

- **Fats & Oils** – Saturated fats, hydrogenated oils, margarine and corn oil.

- **Meat, Poultry & Fish** – Pork, lamb, beef, chicken, turkey, crustaceans, other seafood except the cold water fish listed above.

- **Convenience Foods** – Sweets, chocolate, artificial sweeteners, microwave meals, tinned foods, powdered soups, instant meals, fast food takeaways.

- **Drinks** – Coffee, fizzy drinks, tea, beer, wine, milk, fruit juice, dairy smoothies and liqueurs.

- **Dairy Products** – Milk, eggs, cheese, cream, yoghurt and ice cream.

- **Others** – Vinegar, white pasta, white bread, wholemeal bread, biscuits, soy sauce, Tamari, Condiments (tomato sauce, mayonnaise etc).

General Guidance

Stick to salads, fresh vegetables and healthy nuts and oils. Try to consume plenty of raw foods and at least 2-3 litres of water daily.

Try to stay clear of fatty meats, cheese, sweets, chocolates, alcohol and tobacco. Packaged foods are often full of hidden offenders and microwave meals are full of sugars and salts. Over cooking also removes all of the nutrition from a meal.

Losing Weight

Samantha came along to me to lose weight. She had been struggling with her weight for years and desperately wanted to get into her size 12 jeans again. She is in her early twenties, stands five feet six inches tall and was a size 16. Samantha has been following a low fat diet and walking three times a week, but didn't seem to be losing weight.

Her lifestyle was pretty hectic and she was always 'eating on the go'. She tried to eat low fat options but never felt completely satisfied and often wanted chocolate and sweets – which she succumbed to, at some point during the day. She thinks there is something wrong with her because she does not believe she has the will power to stay away from chocolate. I tell her that she is wrong and she has just not found the right strategy yet.

By late afternoon, every day, Samantha is shattered and her energy levels are extremely low. Samantha wants to feel energised and better about herself, as well as lose her excess weight and the appetite for sugary foods.

Samantha can't understand why she is not losing weight, as although she is eating sweets or chocolate every day, she reckons her calorie content for a day is only around 1500 calories, which is less than the recommended average. So where is she going wrong?

I explain to Samantha that although she is eating less calories than most people, she is actually eating the wrong sort of foods. Samantha eats a lot of low fat products – such as low fat ice cream, low fat salad dressings, low fat cookies, diet coke, artificial sweeteners in the tea and coffee etc. Although this might look like the sensible thing to do (cutting back on fats) most low fat products have extra sugar added to them to ensure they still taste good. And this extra sugar is what is causing her to gain body fat! Any sugar put into our bodies causes your body to secrete insulin. This rise in insulin will convert into fat, any sugar not immediately used for energy – and thus we get excess fat in our bodies.

Diets high in sugar based products alter the acidity/alkalinity balance of the body, moving the body into a state of chaos. Fat is then stored away to help protect the organs from the excess acid in the body. This makes us unhealthy and tired.

The best way to lose excess body fat is to start alkalising our bodies by eating more alkalising food and cutting back on the sugary/acid forming foods. I started by advising Samantha to stop eating so many low fat/high sugary foods. This meant cutting out foods with artificial sweeteners in them and cutting back on ready meals (which are incredibly sugary). I advised her to start planning her meals more, so that she didn't have to eat convenience foods so much. I asked her to start eating more of the alkaline forming foods and to cut down on chocolate and sweets.

Samantha started snacking more on seeds, nuts, raisins and oat cakes which were less acid forming and more healthy. She also started to eat more vegetables and have a wheatgrass drink every day to help alkalise her system. Within a few days, Samantha noticed the difference not only in her energy levels but also her trousers were starting to feel looser.

This spurred Samantha on to carry on with her healthy eating approach and also gave her the energy and motivation to do more exercise. I started personal training Samantha and within just a few weeks her body shape and fitness improved significantly. Three months on and she is a size 12, and she is energetic and happy. She also does not crave sugary foods. Alkalise your body if you want to lose weight!

Eating Sensibly

Don't combine proteins and refined carbohydrates in a meal, as this will slow down your digestion. A slow digestion will also make it more difficult for your body to eliminate waste, and so will make you feel sluggish. Proteins are foods such as meat, fish, dairy produce, cheese, yoghurt and milk. Refined carbohydrates are foods such as potatoes, bread, pasta, rice and couscous.

Aim to have a refined carbohydrate *or* a portion of protein with a green leaf salad or vegetables for your main meal. For instance, have pasta or rice with vegetable sauce and salad or stir fried vegetables. Have some chicken or fish with vegetables or salad. Instead of taking sandwiches to school or work, take a salad with some protein, such as meat, tuna, cheese etc. Remember that 70% of your plate should be made up of greens, to help alkalise you!

Aerobic Exercise

Aerobic exercise is exercising with oxygen, and is fantastic for your health and fitness. When you are aerobically fit, your body more efficiently takes in and uses oxygen to sustain movement more easily. Aerobic exercise will make you feel and look great. It will help you to shed any excess body fat and will increase your endorphins.

Achieving a higher level of aerobic fitness can be fun because there are so many activities to choose from. Among the many options are: walking, dancing, swimming, cycling, cross-country skiing, running, jogging, skipping, aquatic aerobics, aerobics, stair climbing and rowing. Walking is a popular form of aerobic exercise. It's simple and cheap, and all you need is a pair of comfortable walking shoes. Live longer and stay healthier with just 30 minutes' exercise a day.

REASONS TO EXERCISE

- ♥ Reduces stress

- ♥ Produces endorphins (so you feel fabulous!)

- ♥ Reduces weight and fat

- ♥ Increases immunity

- ♥ Prevents heart disease

- ♥ Lowers cholesterol levels

- ♥ Prevents osteoporosis

- ♥ Prevents back problems

- ♥ Prevents diabetes

- ♥ Strengthens bones and joints

Aerobic exercise cannot be overlooked. It can help you live longer and live healthier. Exercise is good for you!

Excessive Exercise

Exercising makes you feel more vibrant and alive. However, if you exercise to excess, this will make you feel drained and burnt out.

Some people over-exercise because they are so desperate to shift the last few pounds of excess weight that they are carrying. If you exercise too much, you will create excess lactic acid in your body. Lactic acid is a toxin and can cause harm to our organs and cells. In order to protect your vital organs, your body will hold on to any excess body fat to protect these from this acid. This is why you are unable to shift those last few pounds. Make sure that you are sensible with the amount of exercise you do. If you are constantly tired and not shifting the last bit of body fat, then you need to reassess how much exercise you are doing. After exercising, make sure you have a green drink to help alkalise your system.

Exercising correctly is important too. If you are exercising with pain, then you are not doing it aerobically. Exercise at a comfortable speed, so that you are still able to hold a conversation with someone. Always do a 10-12 minute warm-up period, where you gradually increase your heart rate. Do an activity at a pace well below your optimum training heart rate (such as a slow jog, if you plan to run or a slow walk before a fast walk.) The warm-up will give the body time to adjust, so that it can mobilise fats, helping you to be a better fat burner.

After your warm up and warm up stretches, exercise aerobically for 20-30 minutes at your optimal heart rate. This is calculated by subtracting your age from the number 180.

180 – _____ (*Your age*) = _____ Beats per minute.

Do a proper warm down after this session. This should last for about 10 minutes. Gradually decrease the intensity and speed to reduce your heart rate. Finish off stretching all major muscle groups.

Exercising properly will ensure that you are burning fat as your fuel and not just using sugars. It will also help you to become more aerobically fit.

Resistance Training

Resistance training is great because it not only helps you to improve your strength but it also really helps to shape your body and give you the look that you desire. Resistance training needs only to be done 2-3 times a week and is something that you should talk to a gym trainer or personal trainer about, so that they can design you a safe and effective programme that will give you the dramatic results that you want.

> **WARNING:** If you have never exercised regularly before, or have not been active for some time, have a health condition or are seriously overweight, then please build up very slowly to 30 minutes a day. Always check with your doctor if you have any doubts.

Cigarettes & Drugs

These are simple – "no". They deplete your body of nutrients that you need for good health. Anything that takes oxygen away from your cells, such as cigarettes, is going to affect your health negatively. Cigarettes and drugs are severe toxins for your body and will not help you to feel more healthy and energetic.

Alcohol

Alcohol instantly kills brain cells as it destroys the oxygen levels in the brain. It also stops digestion. Drink little alcohol to remain healthy. Binge drinking will not help your health or wellbeing.

Get the body, mind and health you deserve by looking after yourself *now*. Change some of your lifestyle habits and behaviours and you will look and feel fantastic!

♥ ♥ ♥ **Self-Coaching Session** ♥ ♥ ♥

Answer the following questions to see what steps you need to take *now*, to get the life, energy and body that you deserve.

Oxygen

What are you going to do to increase your oxygen flow?

_____

_____

_____

Water

How much water are you currently drinking every day?

_____

What other drinks do you drink during the day?

_____

_____

_____

Write down a list of everything that you've drunk today.

_____

_____

_____

_____

_____

How often do you eat when you're probably thirsty?

_____

How will drinking more water help you to stay healthy?

_____

_____

Alkalising

How much of your diet is made up of water? (Remember water is in salads, vegetables and fruit.)

_____

_____

What do you need to do to alkalise your body more?

_____

_____

When will you commit to doing it?

_____

_____

What is your PH level?

_____

_____

Exercise

How often do you exercise?

_____

_____

Do you do a proper warm up and cool down?

_____

_____

What exercise could you do that would be fun?

_____

_____

_____

_____

How could you make exercise more pleasurable?

_____

_____

_____

_____

Do you want to feel more energetic?

_____

_____

Self Coaching for Health & Wellbeing

This is a self-coaching session to help you come up with ways to transform your life.

G is for Goal

On a scale of 1 -10 where 10 is "outstanding health and wellbeing", where are you?

_____

❤ What would make it a 10?

_____

_____

❤ Think about having outstanding health and wellbeing and take yourself forward to a point in time when you feel both of these. What do you notice that shows you that you have this? Or how do you know this has happened?

_____

_____

❤ What are you doing that shows you have outstanding health and wellbeing?

_____

_____

❤ What are you hearing that tells you have outstanding health and wellbeing?

_____

_____

❤ How are you feeling at this point in the future?

_____

_____

❤ What are you saying to yourself?

_____

_____

_____

_____

R is for Reality

❤ What is going on right now that tells you, you don't have outstanding health and wellbeing?

_____

_____

❤ What have you done so far to improve things?

_____

_____

❤ What were the obstacles you met from doing these things?

_____

_____

_____

💜 What obstacles or possible barriers are in your way that stops you from moving forward?

_____

_____

_____

💜 What do you need to do to help you to have outstanding health and wellbeing?

_____

_____

💜 Are there any resources that might help you?

_____

_____

_____

O is for Options

💜 What could you do to move yourself just one step forward now?

_____

_____

💜 Go wild and write down as many ways that you can think of to have outstanding health and wellbeing.

_____

_____

_____

_____

💜 What else could you do if you didn't have to explain what you were doing or be answerable to anybody?

_____

_____

_____

❤ If you could devote all your time to having outstanding health and wellbeing, what would you do then?

_____

_____

_____

❤ If you went to your guardian angel for help what might she suggest?

_____

_____

❤ What could you do, if money was unlimited, to have outstanding health and wellbeing?

_____

_____

❤ If you secretly know what you should do first, what would it be?

_____

_____

❤ Read back carefully through your options. Check to see if any of them spark another idea that you might consider?

_____

_____

❤ Choose one of the options that you think would be right for you to do now. Circle it.

❤ If you do the one thing that you have chosen, will it move you forward? If not choose something else.

_____

❤ How will this option make you healthier?

_____

_____

_____

W is for Will

💜 What are you going to do?

_____

_____

_____

_____

💜 What will you do? List the actions that you can take now to make you healthier.

_____

_____

_____

_____

_____

💜 How will these actions allow you to be healthier?

_____

_____

💜 When are you going to take these actions? In what time scale?

_____

_____

💜 How long do you think this will take you?

_____

_____

💜 Should anybody else be involved in this list of actions?

_____

_____

_____

💜 What do you want this person, or these people, to do?

_____

_____

_____

💜 When will you tell them?

_____

_____

_____

💜 Who else should know that you are doing these things?

_____

_____

_____

💜 When will you tell them?

_____

_____

_____

💜 Whatever your first step is, can you think of any obstacle that might stop you from doing it?

_____

_____

_____

💜 How likely is it to stop you? If likely, what can you do to make your first step more achievable?

_____

_____

_____

_____

💜 How will you overcome this obstacle?

_____

_____

_____

💜 What will you do to stop it from stopping you?

_____

_____

_____

💜 Is there anything else you need to consider before you begin?

_____

_____

_____

💜 On a scale of 1-10 where 10 is "I am totally committed to having outstanding health and wellbeing and taking action", where are you?

_____

_____

_____

💜 If you are not a 10 – what do you need to do to make it a 10?

_____

_____

_____

Chapter Ten

Putting it all Together – Sharing my Secret with You

*Your quick reference guide
to feeling fantastic.*

In this Chapter you will:

- Put every thing together that you have learnt so far
- Learn the 5 quick steps to feeling amazing *every day*
- Learn to meditate
- *Have your life transformed!*

Putting it all Together - Sharing my Secret with You

Throughout this book, you have learnt how to make yourself feel fantastic, every day. You are in control of your feelings and you are the master of your own destiny. By imagining and knowing what you want to feel like, look like, what you want your relationships to be like and what you want to make happen in your life, you will ensure that you live a life that is fulfilling and exciting.

These last few pages of this book will reveal to you, in quick simple steps, how to feel amazing every day and stay this way. Enjoy!

💜 💜 💜 YOUR QUICK REFERENCE GUIDE TO FEELING FANTASTIC 💜 💜 💜

💜 **Only say nice things about yourself and others**. *Imagine & You Can…*

💜 **Always smile and be happy**. *Imagine & You Can…*

💜 **Always praise yourself**, even when you haven't done something quite how you wanted to have done it. Still love yourself. You are not always perfect or you would not have the opportunity to grow. And growing is essential in life. Remember when a plant ceases to grow it dies – don't do the same! Live and grow! *Imagine & You Can…*

💜 **Don't scare yourself about what might or might not happen**. Focus on the positive ALWAYS. *Imagine & You Can…*

💜 **Face challenges head on and learn from them**. Praise yourself for doing things that other people don't have the courage to do. *Imagine & You Can…*

💜 **Recall only the good things that people have said to you**. Polluting your mind with unhelpful or negative comments will not serve you. Dismiss any harsh or negative comments now. *Imagine & You Can…*

💜 **Believe in yourself**. Support & nurture yourself. Only YOU can make a real difference to your life. *Imagine & You Can…*

💜 **Be prepared to do what it takes to feel good and live the life that you want**. Take positive actions and steps every day to create the life that you want. *Imagine & You Can…*

💜 **Surround yourself with positive people who are inspiring and uplifting**. *Imagine & You Can…*

♥ **Take care of your body and mind every day**. Be Sure to breathe properly, exercise regularly, drink plenty of water, alkalise your body and eat the right foods. *Imagine & You Can...*

♥ **Be kind to your mind**. Say only good things to yourself to make yourself feel good. Imagine only nice things happening in your life. Treat your mind with love and guard it closely. Create an early morning routine for your mind, to make you feel fabulous every morning. *This MUST be the most important routine of all. Prepare your mind for an excellent day and you will see how your life changes within days. Imagine & You Can...*

Your Mind Morning Routine

Imagine every morning that you are having a wonderful day and feeling happy and full of life. You can! I am now going to share with you my secret to feeling spectacular. Every morning, follow the series of five steps, listed below, to have an awe-inspiring day.

By giving your mind time *every* morning you will feel fabulous. Although you might rather stay in bed... *Get Up!* Make it a *must* to get up 30-45 minutes earlier, so you set up your day in a tremendous way which will make dramatic changes to your life. If needs be, go to bed 30-45 minutes earlier so you still get the same amount of sleep. By getting up earlier, you will have uninterrupted free time as everyone else will be fast asleep, to train your mind to feeling splendid.

Are you ready? Here are the five steps:

 **Step One** ♥ ♥ ♥

Positive Thoughts & Affirmations

Create a list of affirmations and positive thoughts that you can say out aloud to yourself, as soon as you wake up, to inspire you and lift your early morning mood. Be proactive and make yourself feel great.

The greatest among us were not satisfied with the way things were. Think Ghandi. Think Mother Teresa, Bill Gates, Einstein, Mandela. All these people gave themselves time to think and dream of what they wanted in life. They created in their minds what they wanted to happen. They believed in themselves and believed that they could make a difference in the world – and they did. Believe that you can make a difference in the world and in your own life. Believe in yourself. Build yourself up now and talk to yourself in a kind way, to give yourself the drive and momentum to create wonderful things in your life. Great leaders understand the power of thoughts and allowing themselves time to have great thoughts. Immerse yourself with the same power. Give yourself ten minutes every morning where you can really focus on good thoughts and positive affirmations to set your day up to be a victory.

When you go into the bathroom, instead of looking at yourself in the mirror and putting yourself down, say "hello" to yourself. Say you love yourself and that you are wonderful and that today is going to be a fantastic day. Don't wait for others to build you up, instead boost yourself up with loving and kind words.

❤ ❤ ❤ Step Two ❤ ❤ ❤

Be Grateful & Ask Good Questions

Every morning, take five minutes to practise being grateful about your life. By thinking about and saying out loud all the things that you feel grateful about, you will instantly start to feel great. Think about all the people in your life whom you love and whom you are grateful for. Think about all the things that you have and do, that you are grateful for. And most of all be grateful that you are alive and that you are you. Just keep saying thank you and feel that glow and warmth grow inside your heart. It is a wonderful feeling.

Ask yourself good questions to also make you feel wonderful. Ask yourself questions that will put you in the right frame of mind and make your day better and your relationships better with yourself and others. "What can I do today to make it a wonderful day?" or "How can I show my friends and family I love them?" or "What can I do today to show love to myself?" Always ask questions that will move you into a great frame of mind.

❤ ❤ ❤ Step Three ❤ ❤ ❤

Visualise & Plan

Visualise what you want to happen today and then plan it. Think about the outcomes that you want and what you want to achieve. Visualise any meetings with work colleagues, friends and family and how you want these to unfold. Set up your day and design it how you want it. Every person who has achieved great things uses vision to create their outcomes. Know what you want and then take action to make it the way you want it.

 **Step Four**

Have Role Models & Read Positive Words

Set aside 15 minutes every morning to allow time to read self development and self help books. By reading and hearing the inspiring words of great authors you will be immersing yourself in wise and uplifting thoughts that will excite you and not hinder you. Choose books to read where you will be positively influenced by good role models. People such as Gandhi and Buddha have wise words to raise your spirits. There are numerous authors in the self help genre who are incredibly inspiring. I have learnt so much from so many authors. Louise Hay offers sound advice and incitement into self-love and healing; Anthony Robbins' books and CDs help you to find your personal power; Paul McKenna helps you to overcome issues with the power of the mind and NLP; Barbara De Angelis and John Gray have some fantastic books on relationships; Sondra Ray has a great selection of books on the importance of beliefs for relationships and losing weight. There are literally thousands and thousands of great books that are worth reading. Become someone who wants to learn and grow. Have breakfast with these authors and learn from their knowledge and wise words. Feed your mind with happiness, hope and excitement.

 **Step Five**

Meditate to Feel Inspired

By starting the day off with meditation, you will feel instantly more balanced and you will set yourself up well for the day. The physical benefits of meditation have been well documented. It lowers the blood pressure, pulse rate, and the level of stress hormones in the body. It helps both the body and mind feel rejuvenated and helps people live longer and better lives. These are fantastic reasons in themselves to meditate. But I think the main thing I have discovered with meditating is the ability to not only feel peaceful and harmonious but also to feel incredibly inspired.

Meditating enables you to release any tension that you may be carrying. It allows you to create a peaceful state within yourself, one where you feel at ease but also excited. When you meditate you quieten your mind. This might initially be difficult for many people – it definitely was for me, as all sorts of chatter came up in my mind. However, if you keep practising, you will find your mind naturally starts to quieten. When you allow this to happen, it is often at these points that a fabulous idea just pops up in your head. This is simply because your mind is quiet and the energy waves can now be easily picked up by your subconscious mind and then miraculously transferred to your conscious mind. It is amazing. I have had some of my best ideas in this quiet state.

Try it and see what wonderful ideas suddenly pop into your mind. Everyone can meditate, it is easy. All you have to do is to sit quietly, close your eyes, and take a few deep breaths. The body will automatically relax. You can repeat the words "peace" or "love" or anything that is meaningful to you that will make you feel good and also quieten your mind. Maybe you could even say "I love myself" or even ask yourself a question silently, such as "What is it I need to know?" Then just sit there quietly. Answers may come immediately or in a day or two. Don't feel rushed. Allow your mind the space to let the thoughts and ideas flow.

You cannot meditate incorrectly and any starting point is perfect for you. You can find books and CDs that will teach you different methods and there are many classes around, too. If you are new to meditation, I would suggest that you begin with only five minutes at a time so that you don't get bored. But just these five minutes will give you tremendous motivation and inspiration to your life. There is a tremendous wisdom inside all of us. All the answers are inside us, you just need to ask the right questions and wait for the answers.

Give yourself this gift and see your life transform

Now that you have your five positive steps to make a real difference to your mind – step to it.

FIVE POSITIVE STEPS

💜 Affirmations & Positive Thoughts: **5-10 minutes**

💜 Gratitude & Good Questions: **5 minutes**

💜 Visualise & Plan Your Day: **5 minutes**

💜 Read a Positive Book: **10-15 minutes**

💜 Meditate: **5-10 minutes**

This routine will take you around 30-40 minutes and will transform your life. I swear by this!

Always make sure you work on yourself every day to feel fabulous. Continually check in with yourself. By constantly monitoring and focusing on increasing your good feelings you will feel fantastic.

I hope that *Imagine & You Can* has given you as much pleasure reading it and working on yourself, as it has given to me when writing it.

Know that my support is always with you, and more importantly remember *you can create the life and the feelings that you want.* Focus daily on what you want and always imagine what you want.... *Imagine & You Can!!*

Have fun, be happy and have love for everyone.

Davinia

If you would like to contact me personally then I would love to hear from you.

*See me at **www.davinia.org.uk***

*Email me at **dg@davinia.org.uk***

Recommended Reading

Ageless Body, Timeless Mind, by Deepak Chopra

Awaken the Giant Within, by Anthony Robbins

Change Your Life in Seven Days, by Paul Mckenna

Constant Craving: What Your Food Cravings Means and How To Overcome Them, by Dorren Virtue

Everyday Wisdom, by Wayne Dyer

Feel the Fear and Do It Anyway, by Susan Jeffers

Fit for life, by Harvey and Marilyn Diamond

Instant Confidence, by Paul Mckenna

Man's Search For Meaning, by Viktor Frankl

Manifest Your Destiny, by Wayne Dyer

Many Lives, Many Masters, by Brian Weiss

Meditation, by Brian Weiss

Perfect Health, by Deepak Chopra

Real Magic, byWayne Dyer

Screw It, Let's Do It, by Richard Branson

Slow Burn, by Stu Mittleman

Secrets About Men Every Woman Should Know, by Barbara De Angleis

Staying on the Path, by Wayne Dyer

Time for a Change, by Richard Bandler

The Breakthrough Experience, by Dr. John Demartini

The Cosmic Ordering Service, by Barbel Mohr

The Definitive Book of Body Language, by Allan & Barbara Pease

The Key, by Joe Vitale

The Riches Within, by Dr. John Demartini

The 12 Stages of Healing, by Donald Epstein

The Optimum Nutrition Bible, by Patrick Holford

The Greatness Guide, by Robin Sharma

You Can Heal Your Life, by Louise Hay

You Can Have What You Want, by Michael Neill

Your sacred self, by Wayne Dyer

Zero Limits, by Joe Vitale

48 Hours To a Healthier Life, by Suzi Grant

About Davinia Gill

Davinia Gill runs a personal training and coaching practice for women. She combines her personal training, coaching and NLP therapy to help her clients achieve outstanding health and fitness and wellbeing.

Davinia practises what she preaches and is passionate about what she does. She is totally committed to ensuring that her clients achieve the results that they want and deserve in life.

She has been in the health and fitness industry for over ten years, working with many clients to help them take control of their lives physically, with the right nutrition and exercise.

Davinia is a fully certified personal performance coach and personal trainer and has also trained in NLP on Paul McKenna courses. Her passion for both, led her to realize that anything in life is possible and that young women can transform their lives to be happy and fulfilled. Sharing this message was the motivation behind *Imagine & You Can*.

In her spare time, Davinia loves spending time with her fiancé, Paul. She loves running, walking, working out at the gym, socializing with friends and family, reading self development books and going on lovely holidays!

You can learn more about Davinia's services and products at www.davinia.org.uk

---

QUALIFICATIONS

- Diploma in Personal Training: Level 3 Fully qualified YMCA Personal Trainer

- Antenatal and Postnatal Fitness Trainer

- Sports Conditioning Trainer

- Technique and Improvements Trainer in Running

- Nutrition and Weight Management Coach

- Diploma in Personal Performance Coaching: Professional Coach, trained by the Coaching Academy

- Licensed Master Practitioner of NLP, trained by Paul Mckenna, Richard Bandler and Michael Neil

- Hypnosis Practitioner, trained by Paul Mckenna and Richard Bandler

In loving memory of Helwyn Wood
who lost her fight with cancer on 17th July 2009.

Her positive and grateful attitude will live on in others.